THE EXPAT MARRIAGE GUIDEBOOK

THE EXPAT MARRIAGE GUIDEBOOK

Surviving and Thriving in an Overseas Relationship

ASHLINN ROMAGNOLI

Adam Lofbomm

La Coppia Utopia

Contents

To my mother, Cynthia Rae Romagnoli, who died of breast cancer in 2009. She would probably have loved Adam even more than she loved me, but only slightly less than she would have loved shoving a copy of this book into the hands of every stranger she met.

Although, to be honest, my mom never did meet a stranger.

Introduction

Hello, stranger.

If you're taking a look at this book, chances are that you're either married or living in a foreign country. Maybe you're even doing (or considering doing) both at once, which makes you both audacious and foolhardy—maybe even a bit brazen. My kinda person, but if that's the road you've chosen to travel, you might want to consider picking up a guidebook. Fortunately for you, you've already got one in hand!

Travel is an interesting word, one that, for so many of us, evokes a general sense of excitement, wonder... maybe a touch of apprehension. Not unlike marriage, when you get right down to it. After all, what is marriage but a journey?

Just as I was beginning to pull out ye olde cross-stitching materials to emblazon this adage on a pillow or a cat bed or something—my own twist on the LIVE LAUGH LOVE motto I loathe with a depth usually reserved for people who clip their toenails on the subway—curiosity led me to look up the etymology of the word "travel."

As it turns out, "travel" is an alteration of the Middle English *travelen*, meaning "to toil, work," and the Old French *travailler*, which is even worse: "to trouble, suffer, be worn out."[1]

That is *not* the vibe the innumerable travel-related instagram hashtags had sold me, but the more I thought about it, the more sense it made.

The fact is that despite its many charms and benefits, traveling is *hard*. In addition to all its wonders and excitement, it can be unbearably stressful and can make us feel foolish, ignorant, and small. By leaving our comfort zones, we are often faced with coming to terms with who we really are as individuals. This can be a wonderful thing, but it can also be earth-shattering.

In a word, travel *exposes* you in a way that little else does—except maybe marriage.[2]

In the end, I was more right than I'd originally known: being married *is* just like traveling. It's just that it's both the beautiful version with impeccably chosen filters *and* the gritty reality all wrapped up into one.

And that's why I wrote this book. Because as it turns out, embarking upon two of the most drastic and stressful changes a human being can experience (namely, moving and marrying) at the same time gives a person a serious crash course in building a relationship that is resilient, reciprocal, and fulfilling.

For individuals trying to build a relationship with either a person not from their native culture or in a place that is not their native home (or both!), it's particularly important to approach your relationship with patience, generosity, and open-heartedness.

I've divided the book into two sections: Strategy and Tactics, with the hope that both the macro-level approach to relationships and the micro-level practical day to day tips will be useful as you navigate these waters. You can read the whole thing in order, or jump straight to the chapters that call out to you.

With all its hard work, messiness, and unexpected turns, I delight in my relationship with Adam daily. That's what I want for everyone who reads this book, which I know sounds incredibly cheesy, but it's actually quite selfish. Perhaps the only irrefutable fact of the universe is that the genuinely good stuff—kindness, generosity, and, of course, love—only multiplies, never subtracts. The more love and care there is in this universe, the better off we all are for it.

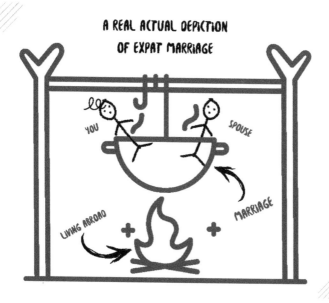

A REAL ACTUAL DEPICTION
OF EXPAT MARRIAGE

About the Authors

I know, I know, usually About the Author is but a sparse paragraph tacked at the end of the book, and including a whole up front section feels a little, I don't know... indulgent?

But this is a book of relationship advice forged specifically in the fires of my marriage, so I figured it would be a good idea to give you the quick and dirty of who we are as individuals as well as a little background on our relationship.

Adam and I kicked off our lives together during the last big trip we took before the pandemic hit. It was December 2019, and as we walked through the streets of Tokyo at four in the morning (jet lag is a bitch), I remember looking down at my tennis shoes and then at the man next to me, and realizing that I wanted to spend the rest of my life doing *this* with *this person*. We had both traveled extensively in our lives: I am what is known as a third culture kid (raised in Japan and Germany & later studied in England) and Adam spent a decade of his adult life in South Korea.

I remember being so nervous about it: we hadn't been dating very long and we both had relationship histories that merited serious consideration (more on that later). But we talked extensively about our feelings and intentions that morning on the Toyosu Ohashi Bridge, and got engaged a month later on our one-year dating anniversary, full of plans to uproot our lives and begin living a more nomadic lifestyle.

Well, you know what they say about plans.

Not two months later, our world was irrefutably altered from the life our hopes and dreams had sketched out: The pandemic had stilled the world and kicked off an era of global uncertainty and fear, a tornado had ravaged my neighborhood and house, I'd lost my job as an account supervisor for an ad agency, and I underwent surgery for endometriosis in a hospital locked down by COVID-19. It was a frightening time, to say the least.

Still, although weathering all of those storms at once (in addition to a family death a little later that summer) was exhausting and frightening, one bright side was that it acted as a crucible. It turned what had previously been a hunch that we were choosing the right life partner into a much stronger hypothesis.

Yet I at least was still incredibly nervous about making such a huge decision, so we went to our relationship counselor to hash out some of our anxious questions about our impending marriage. He metaphorically bopped us on the heads for looking for the kind of guarantees that simply do not exist in this version of the universe: you can never really *know* what a marriage will be like until you're in it. At some point, you just have to leap.

So leap we did—we eloped in September of 2020 (partly to avoid any question of family traveling for the event and potentially putting themselves at risk of COVID-19 and partly because elopement is kind of our style) and began planning our move away from the United States, which shifted from a plan to move every two months to experience a variety of countries to a decision to simply relocate to Italy, where I have citizenship.

It's important to note that at this point in time the world had cautiously re-opened after the initial wave of COVID-19 throughout the summer and early autumn of 2020. Governments in much of the world, particularly Europe, had cracked open their doors for visitors, but little did we know that additional variants and waves would rear their ugly heads periodically (and still do at the time this book went to print). In retrospect, this was not the simplest time to move, but of course, as they say, hindsight is twenty-twenty.

We fixed up my tornado-swept house to rent; sold most of our possessions; and made our way with six suitcases, a portable recording booth, and our two sweet cats to Europe. We landed in Rome with just one day to spare before the second lock-down kept us all cooped up again—this time, in a country with which we were almost entirely unfamiliar where everyone spoke a language that we understood even less.

In many ways, commencing our life as a married couple while simultaneously moving overseas during a pandemic amplified all of our experiences a hundredfold, like deciding to finally learn how to fly a plane only after the pilot has passed out in the cabin or waltzing onto a stage after a few drinks with nothing but a harmonica and a dream.[3] It forced us to come to terms with ourselves, each other, and our marriage with stark, unrelenting honesty.

The word *marriage*—much like *travel*, as noted in the intro-duction—can conjure up wildly different mental images: there are probably as many different definitions of commitment and marriage as there are couples. For us, marriage is a public and legally binding way to affirm our love; *love* being, as bell hooks describes in her incredible book *All About Love*, "a mix [of] various ingredients—care, affection, recognition, respect, commitment, and trust, as well as honest and open communication."

Despite the precarious situation we put ourselves in, somehow Adam and I live every day of our lives wrapped up in the context of a happy and healthy marriage. Well, maybe not "somehow"... it has taken a *lot* of work, both together and separately, to be here; it's work that literally never ends.

But the fact is that this relationship is the most worthwhile work either of us have ever undertaken. The rewards have been beyond even the wildest dreams I nursed standing on that bridge in Tokyo over four years ago, so we have decided to share our best advice and observations about being married—particularly for our fellow expats who are juggling all kinds of unique problems in addition to managing a relationship.

But Just Who Are You Two, Anyway?

Well, that would take a whole book on its own to dive into. If you're really curious and good at googling, you can find out all kinds of stuff about us on the internet, like how Adam used to run an art gallery and I was once a fire warden at Carnegie Hall.[4] But here's a cheat sheet:

ASHLINN

Enneagram Type: 8w7 "The Maverick" or "The Non-Conformist" Horoscope: Capricorn/Aquarius cusp. Essentially a goofier, weirder version of a Capricorn. Hide your kids. Hide your wife.

Three Words To Describe Myself: Tenacious, light-hearted, conscientious

Profession: Project manager, voice actor, and now a writer, too!

Dream Job: Crotchety novelist

Deadly Sin: Pride

Most Annoying Trait (according to Self): When temper is finally ignited, it's pretty vengeful, and I hate how vulnerable that makes me feel

Most Annoying Trait (according to Adam): How okay with her own flaws Ash is // being an ice queen

Best Relationship Trait: Maintaining chill

Worst Relationship Trait: Gets impatient with diving too deeply/frequently into feelings

Favorite Things: BOOKS, wine with friends, healthy boundaries, Adam & Z, nests, bees

ADAM

Enneagram Type: 4 wing 3 "The Aristocrat" or "The Enthusiast"

Horoscope: Aries Sun, Virgo Moon, Leo Rising (Adam is way more into horoscopes than I am)

Three Words: Curious, creative, connective

Profession: Voice actor

Dream Job: Creating beautiful spaces

Deadly Sin: Pride (and Gluttony too)

Most Annoying Trait (according to Self): Lack of focus and follow-through

Most Annoying Trait (according to Ashlinn): Forgetting Ash is on his team

Best Relationship Trait: Emotional vulnerability/awareness

Worst Relationship Trait: Too much emotional vulnerability/ awareness

Favorite Things: Enjoying tasty meals with friends, grooving to good tunes, visiting stimulating museums, perusing used book stores, taking motorcycle trips, nerding out on the latest tech, capturing images for making art.

Foreword

Since this book was written pretty much entirely by me, Ash-linn (with Adam's keen ears listening, commenting, and suggesting, of course), we thought it would be fun for Adam to write a little foreword. Little did I know that it would be incredibly poignant and probably render the rest of the book obsolete, but here we are.

Dear reader,

I was born a lover.

From the age of three or four I started pining for a partner to love passionately and to love me back in kind. When my friends and I would play make-believe about Star Wars or G.I Joe, I would inevitably craft some sort of romantic subplot with my imaginary other in the mantle of Princess Leia or Lady Jaye.

By the age of six or seven, I was already over waiting for my love to show up. "Alright already, where is she?"

The love songs of the 60s my mom played in the car first gave poetic voice to my longings, then it was the melancholic lyrics of Brit-pop bands, and after that the refined refrains of Rumi, Neruda, and Rilke. I was convinced I might have to travel the whole world over just to find her out there, and would do so gladly if that is what it would take.

That intense drive to find my person didn't ever leave me. It shaped my life: with my choice of college to be near my first love who I was sure I would marry (only to break up right before first semester), in marrying another one at twenty-five—far too young, thanks to religious/cultural pressure, and then diving into a deeply-damaging rebound marriage in Korea that ended with me becoming twice-divorced within three years' time.

Fail fast, fail often, as they say in Silicon Valley, eh?

Despite all of those misadventures in partnership, I somehow never lost my deep and abiding faith that finding one whom I could share life and love with would be well worth the work.

And work, I found, was exactly what it would take. Work that I hadn't done previously.

Although I had dabbled in personal therapy, and done some couples counseling both before and during the first marriage, I discovered during the codependent, psychologically-scarring shit-show that was my second marriage that I needed to learn to love and commit to myself before I could succeed in loving and committing to someone else.

So, I committed to not commit to anyone else for the next three years. I got some tattoos to signify that commitment, and to remind me never to abandon myself just to not be alone ever again.

I built a new life that I loved, brick by brick. I fed my body and my mind and my heart nourishing food. I invested in coaching and bodywork. I found good people with whom I nurtured quality friendships. I crafted a safe, beautiful home environment that expressed my spirit. I showed up at my men's group for three hours each Wednesday to work out in our emotional gym, building my capacity to feel the feelings I had avoided feeling and to speak the truths I had been afraid to say.

Although I opened my heart to love again after those three incredible years of growth and healing, it took one additional year of searching before Ashlinn Romagnoli finally (alright already!) appeared in my life and transformed it forever.

It sounds cliche to say, I know, but she was worth every minute of those thirty-nine years of waiting, all the relationship failures, and those three years of work on myself— and still would have been worth double all that. Loving her and being loved by her is the deepest and richest experience I have ever known. Together, each day, we get to meditate on how the deep mystery and the banal mundanity of the universe meet in us.

And that she too had a desire to roam far and wide across this beautiful planet of ours, soaking up all of the richness that its various places and cultures and faces have to offer us—my heart almost bursts at the thought of my good fortune to have found such a life partner as this.

It still takes work—on myself and on our relationship—to make this life of ours work. But it is imminently worth the effort, I assure you.

In these pages, dear reader, I hope that you will benefit from the fruits that Ashlinn has carefully plucked from the tree of our life together and so beautifully preserved in this book for you.

If you are still searching for your one to adventure with, may our story give you hope that you can indeed find them. If you have already found a love with whom you can build a life, may these insights give you some means to deepen and enrich your partnership.

Be kind and gentle with yourself. Be kind and gentle with your partner. Be kind and gentle with that third entity that you are nurturing—a life together.

Godspeed on your journey,

Adam Lofbomm

"The privilege of a lifetime is to become who you truly are." – C. G. Jung

Three Brief Notes

A Note on the Terms Immigrants and Expats

There are a number of wonderful and thought-provoking essays and articles about the uses of the word *expat*, a term which has been in the spotlight in recent years as individuals attempt to understand how it has been used and abused to distinguish between "good" immigrants—ie, wealthy, often white individuals —and "bad" immigrants—ie, poor individuals from 'undesirable' countries or backgrounds, including asylum-seekers, often non-white or non-European individuals.

I believe that language is powerful and that we often use it in coded ways to communicate often-distasteful nuance. This has been the case at times with the term *expat*.

Still, I personally consider the term expatriate, or expat, to have an important function. An expat, in my mind, is a person who is temporarily living in a foreign country with no intention to stay permanently or no clear idea of what their next step might be. When I was growing up across Japan and Germany, my family would have fit into this category. Adam felt he was both an expat and an immigrant at different points during his decade spent in South Korea.

Our situation in Italy is a bit confusing. Although I do not feel naturally at home here, I cannot really say I am an immigrant either—I have a passport, family connections, and a lot of privileges as a citizen that immigrants do not—but Adam certainly would say that he is. After all, we are building a home here, and while we cannot say if we'll stay forever, we have no active plans or intentions to leave.

This is all to say that in the course of this book I use *expat* not because I'm ignorant to the very important conversation being had around the terminology defining those who leave their home countries. I partly use it because it's shorter and sounds better with some of the fun phrases we've come up with, like "Expat Tax." But perhaps most importantly, I use it because it is still-standard nomenclature for our audience.

If you're interested in learning more on this topic, I encourage you to seek out additional resources online, particularly from creators of color or diverse backgrounds.

A Note on Our Audience (or: can I read this if I'm not an expat?)

The short answer to this question is an unequivocal *yes*! Hell, you don't even have to be married or dating—this book is written to be interesting and entertaining for anyone who cares about diving deep into human relationships.[5] At least, that's the hope.

While there are many situations and experiences that are unique to expats, the fact is that many of the values and tactics discussed can be used even if you're enjoying life in the same town in which you were born. In fact, sometimes hearing old advice through a new lens ends up being the way it finally sinks in!

Go ahead and read this book—and you can read it in order, if you like, or just bounce around to the chapters that call to you. While there is some method to the madness in ordering, each section stands on its own.

A Note on "La Coppia Utopia"

In case you don't speak Italian, "la coppia utopia" roughly translates to "the utopian couple."

I'm going to come clean right here: it actually doesn't rhyme in Italian (it would be pronounced more like la COppia utoPIA) or really make sense at all. We pronounce it incorrectly—as an English speaker without knowledge of Italian would—so that it does rhyme.

I knew this when I invented the phrase, but the awkwardness is kind of the point: utopia is both a perfect place and a place that doesn't exist.

A good marriage is definitely an utopia, in *both* senses of the word.

PART ONE: STRATEGY

Sun Tzu wrote in the Art of War, "Strategy without tactics is the slowest route to victory. Tactics without strategy is the noise before defeat."

Now, first a caveat that I definitely do *not* believe that love is a battlefield.[6] Still, we can learn a lot from Sun Tzu as we dive into our Guidebook, because a marriage needs an understanding of both the forest and the trees to be successful: both an overarching approach rooted in kindness, generosity, and respect (the strategy) and pragmatic actions that can be put into practice on a day-to-day basis (the tactics).

This first part of the book will focus on the forest—the big picture that creates a foundation upon which you can build.

Alright—enough prologue. Let's dive in!

Make Promises You Can Keep

"I don't feel comfortable promising to love you forever," is probably not a phrase Adam was expecting to hear from me as I wrote our wedding ceremony.

Weddings, after all, are *supposed* to be fluffy and sugary and over-the-top. "I promise to love you" is basically wedding table stakes, like mediocre food and inappropriate speeches uncovering long-buried family drama.[7]

The problem was that I wasn't quite sure how one could promise the continued existence of a feeling. An action? Sure. I hate taking out the organic garbage, but I still make myself do it on the regular. Feelings are famously fickle, feral beasts. They do not put up with being told what to do or where to go. Kinda like a house cat.

The fact is that our world abounds with examples of people who love people who don't love them back, people who love people who are bad for them, and people who love people whom they know that they shouldn't. And trust me: I'm actually grateful for this. Pretty much none of my favorite works of art—be they books, movies, poems, or songs—would exist without the fact that we can't just turn our feelings on and off like a switch.

We can ensure we are open to and ready for loving and being loved. We can make an effort to create an environment that love will find appealing. We can make silly noises and buy its favorite treats and generally make fools of ourselves to attract its attention, but the damned cat still won't do as we say. Sorry—love. I meant that *love* won't do as we say.

Expats need to take particular care when hanging their hats upon this rather unreliable hook of love. I have met a practically uncountable number of individuals whose lives were temporarily or permanently derailed by the right set of gorgeous foreign eyes or a string of poetry whispered in a strange tongue. One stanza in, and suddenly, all bets are off: where we live, what we do for work, how much time we spend on bureaucratic nonsense, what languages we choose to speak are suddenly up in the air in the name of love.

Now, please don't get me wrong: life isn't about always making the "right" choices. Taking risks is an essential part of being human, and I for one will always root for unknown, if not reckless, adventure. This is how we learn and grow. But the kind of commitment that marriage requires isn't easily undone. By all means—extend your year abroad by a month to hit the road with that gorgeous girl you met in Nepal. Book a ticket to meet your German lover in Costa Rica for a warm New Year's getaway. Take the job in Singapore instead of the one in London to see where a strong feeling might take you.

But if you're considering something as (hopefully) permanent as marriage? Best to consider both your decision to marry and the promises you're choosing to make from a more practical standpoint.[8]

It may not be sexy and it may not feel romantic, but it *is* how you can set up a partnership for success. We expats live in a funny little space that manages to be both beyond-your-wildest-dreams amazing and gritty-and-all-too-real at the same time.

You know what? Forget it. I take it back.

Being pragmatic is the *most* romantic thing you can do for your partner, because it is adequately preparing for your road ahead.

Oh, and in case you're wondering what I actually ended up vowing to Adam, since "I promise to love you" was absolutely off the table?

I promised to nurture our love for each other every day.

Now *that*, I can do.

Pick the Right Lunch Buddy

Selecting your ideal life partner is surprisingly similar to picking out lunch, only with far more lasting implications than simply quieting your stomach. Each person—including you— is, in fact, a sandwich. And I mean that as a compliment. Who doesn't like sandwiches?

When you get married, it's kind of like when you're sitting at the lunch table at school and looking to swap halves of a sandwich, only with somewhat higher stakes because you're ostensibly committing to this combination of sandwiches (your half and your partner's) for life.

It might be fun, for example, to enjoy half of a smoked salmon cream cheese bagel with half of a McRib for one day, but is that really the meal you can live with every day for the rest of your life? Don't get me wrong, sometimes unexpected combinations turn out surprisingly well—but just as often, the novelty wears off after a few meals.

Because, you see, you don't get to go to the sandwich shop and order a custom sandwich. You're stuck with whatever options are already available at your table, or maybe one or two over if the kids from other classes aren't complete weirdos. This means that your options may not include something that you would have ordered for yourself.[9]

This means it's important to look very carefully at the qualities of said sandwich. Sandwiches are, broadly speaking, made up of two elements: the fillings and the bread.

Sandwich fillings are, at first glance, the most interesting and appealing part of the whole shebang. There are quite literally infinite varieties of sandwich: tuna melts, French dips, thanksgiving leftovers with cranberry sauce, thanksgiving leftovers *without* cranberry sauce, barbecue tempeh. From a relationship standpoint, the fillings are the attributes and characteristics of a person—things like curiosity, humor, playfulness, kinks. These are the parts of a person that tend to attract us to them in the first place, so they take front and center stage in the day to day experience of a relationship, or when initially choosing what kind of sandwich one wants.

Only the wisest—or perhaps, most experienced—sandwich connoisseurs recognize the absolute indispensability of the bread selection. Rye, cinnamon raisin toast, Wonder Bread, challah—the fact is that the bread is what makes the sandwich, well... a *sandwich*. The bread slices are structural qualities like core values, life goals, approach to finances, and communication or attachment styles. It's true that these are not generally thought of as the sexy parts of the sandwich, but they are mission critical to its construction and continued existence. The bread is what ultimately holds it all together.

A sandwich without the bread is just fillings; and without

quality slices, you basically just have a salad or a mess—not recommended if you want to keep your sandwich delicious for enough time to actually enjoy it. Unfortunately, a lot of people get *really* hung up on the fillings and neglect to scope out the bread their desired fillings are on.

When choosing a partner, people tend to think quite a lot about the fillings, like "do we like the same music?" or "does he enjoy sports?" but kick the can down the road on the structural elements, like how their partner deals with conflict, how many kids they want, where they see themselves living in ten years. These are much harder topics to bring up, of course, but the problem is that these bready issues *always* come up eventually, so it's important to be really, really careful when picking out your lifelong sandwich swap buddy.

The sandwich metaphor is particularly apt for expat relationships: when dating abroad, your array of choices is filled with not just the sammies of your childhood that you are already familiar with, but entirely new varietals or even new takes on the *very concept of the sandwich itself*! Who knows what constitutes a sandwich in foreign lands? A banh mi? A braaibroodjie? Heaven forbid—a *calzone or a hot dog?*[10] And beyond that, the choice to be an expat or not is absolutely a bread quality.

Adam and I may both share an American passport, but we were *absolutely* raised in different cultures: mine, a mishmash that can only be described (without an entire thesis) by the label TCK, third culture kid; his, the American Deep South and all that *that* implies.

While our fillings were deliciously complementary, it became clear that we had some differences when it came to the bread:

expectations around the concept of marriage, for instance, or our understanding of financial health or family responsibility. All things that didn't necessarily need to come up anytime particularly soon in dating, but that we proactively decided to discuss once we felt we were moving toward a more serious future together. Having different breads is perfectly fine... they just have to work well together.

Whether you're meeting someone of a new culture in your home country or meeting someone of your own culture somewhere new—or any of the many permutations in between—**it's absolutely critical to get on the same page about the bread stuff as soon as humanly possible if you're considering being lifelong sandwich buddies.**

Here are a few common questions that expats should answer in three of the most important "bread categories": Family, Language, and Location.

Family

- How will you cope with an unsupportive family if you live abroad?
- Are you expecting that your parents will live with you in your home when they reach a certain age?
- What if a family member in a different country falls ill?
- Is one or are both of you expecting to contribute to your extended family financially?
- Will all of your holidays constitute a return to one of your home countries?
- Are children presumed?[11]

- If you do have kids, how will they be taught about their parents' cultures?

Language

- What will your primary language at home be?
- If you have to choose between your native tongues, how will you acknowledge the disparity there?
- Or are you comfortable communicating entirely in a third language, like my friends who are Turkish and Italian but speak mainly English at home?[12]
- If you have kids, which languages will they speak?

Location

- Perhaps the most critical question for an expat couple— where will you live? In your home country? Your partner's? Or neither?
- Are you going to be expected to follow your partner's job or they yours—making one of you what is known as a "trailing spouse"?
- If you're fundamentally opposed to marriage as an institution (fair enough), would you bend that ideal for visa purposes so your partner can stay with you?

These are not the sexy questions of an expat marriage. They're not the chance meeting, the surprisingly similar humor, the intriguing accent, the curious new mindset, the tantalizing challenge of diving into a culturally diverse relationship. But they *are* some of the most important questions you need to ask when you're at the point of committing to your partner's sandwich for the rest of your life, or at least the foreseeable future.

Fifteen years from now, if you divorce—will you have to stay in this country because otherwise you'd be abandoning your kids? Five years from now, will the way that people religiously recycle to the point of reporting you to your condo board because a single errant milk carton found its way into the mixed trash still be righteous?[13] Ten years from now, will you still be okay struggling to find work because you followed your spouse to their home country and found yourself unable to find meaningful employment—or worse, have you repeatedly left hard-won jobs because your spouse's work keeps them moving? Six months from now, overstaying your intended time in-country by five and a half months, will you still be able to handle the sheer amount of leopard print purporting to be fashion you see on the streets?

By all means—enjoy the fillings. Revel in the fillings. And don't be afraid to *sample* to your heart's content. But when you feel that tug of the heart that suggests that you may have found your person... please, don't forget to think about the bread.

ONE OF THE AUTHOR'S PREFERRED SANDWICHES

WILLING TO LIVE EXPAT LIFE

LIKES TO WALK & TALK

READS BOOKS

V. HOT & GREAT DANCER*

OPEN TO THERAPEUTIC PROCESS

*THIS CARTOON DEFINITELY WASN'T HIJACKED BY ADAM

Unconditional Love Is for Dogs and Babies

There is nothing worse for a marriage than the standard of unconditional love.[14]

For starters, "unconditional love" is kind of an oxymoron in and of itself. Love is a feeling and we can't change our feelings anyway—only the action we take and our perception of what's happening. In this sense, it's not really possible to put conditions on a feeling, only on the expressions of it, making love-the-feeling inherently unconditional. But I digress. The problem isn't actually love being unconditional. It's the *standard* of unconditional love as the most important element in a relationship and the gauge by which we judge our relationships' health.

The problem is that "unconditional love" contains an implicit "no matter what." This is, of course, kind of the point—unconditional love feels like the natural end goal, the obvious antidote to our greatest fears as human beings: that we will end up unloved and abandoned. Simple, right?

Unfortunately, life is *anything* but simple—particularly for expats. In my experience, the idolatry of unconditional love ends up, at best, being a smokescreen that harms our ability to see the truth of our relationships and, at worst, a defense for downright abusive behavior.

The fact is that loving someone should not mean putting up with anything in the name of said love, but that is what frequently ends up happening. When unconditional love is our gauge for relationship health—ie, that the *best* relationships consist of partners who love each other unconditionally—we end up second-guessing ourselves on problems and conflict: is the problem at hand *really* a problem, or is the problem that we just don't love our partner unconditionally enough? That we aren't accepting of exactly who they are?

How many of us have sat on the other end of the phone with a friend embroiled in an objectively horrible relationship only to hear them, weeping, simply say, "...*but I love him/her/them*"?

I know I have, more than once. I've even *been* that person, the one who stayed in a relationship a touch too long because, well, I loved the person, and isn't that the point? As a society, Westerners in particular tend to accept this reasoning. We forgive transgressions because we love them. We excuse neglect because we love them. We stay long after we should because we love them. Because Love Conquers All. Because All You Need Is Love. Because we all want the *best*, and in some fucked-up way we think that if the goal is to love a person *no matter what*, we kinda get extra points if they're more flawed. Right? Doesn't loving like this, against all the odds, kind of make us winners of the love game?

In this way, we find ourselves martyrs to our own relationships, sacrificing happiness for this ideal that, while wonderful for epic poems and songs (and dogs and babies), should never have been a part of the healthy relationship equation in the first place.

Expats especially know what I'm talking about. Expats are the kings, queens, and Grand Viziers of "…but I love them!" Stay in a country you hate? Marry into a culture you can't connect with? Choose a career path you didn't want that allows you to be more flexible? Raise kids somewhere you'd rather not? Give up access to marmite/real tacos/insert homespun joy of your choice? We *love* a good love story, and international relationships generally are that, at the very minimum.

All of those supposedly minor things— the career, the location, the culture—are actually *really important things* for day to day personal happiness, but they somehow sound so insignificant when held up to a goliath of an ideal like *unconditional love.*

Love itself, of course, is an essential element in a marriage. But it is only one of *many, many* ingredients that make up a healthy, happy marriage. It's like the butter in a cookie: you wouldn't want to eat one without it—and you can *tell* when it's not in the recipe—but you can't just have it on its own.[15]

Ultimately, when unconditional love is the standard for relationship health and viability, we trap ourselves into feeling that a failure to love *no matter what*, even if we're miserable, is a reflection of our own failure as a spouse.

The ugly truth is, love isn't enough, and unconditional love is more beautiful in theory than in practice—at least when you're choosing the person you're going to spend every day with for the rest of your life with. And that's okay. It doesn't make you a bad or insufficient partner. It doesn't make you an unromantic person or mean that you can't be silly and giddy and googly-eyed.

It just means that you realize that people are flawed, and when building a partnership, it's okay to acknowledge those flaws—and if they're a problem, you can ask for things to change. It doesn't mean you don't love your partner, just that marriage is a very human—and therefore, also flawed—recipe that needs constant adjustment and work. It means that there are other important ingredients in a cookie, like brown sugar. And chocolate chips.

Ah, hell, I'll just go ahead and share my favorite cookie recipe with you.

ASHLINN'S CHOCOLATE CHIP COOKIE RECIPE

1 1/4 cups* of butter
3/4ish cusp granulated sugar
1ish cup brown sugar
2 eggs
1 teaspoon vanilla extract
1 teaspoon almond extract (SECRET INGREDIENT)
2 3/4 cups flour or a skosh less if you like 'em flatter
1/2 teaspoon salt
2 teaspoons baking soda
2 1/2 - 100 cups of chopped up baking chocolate

PREHEAT OVEN TO 375 F / 190 C

(Don't you hate it when they only tell you to preheat the oven halfway through the recipe and the next step is to put it in the oven but you have to wait?? ...Just me? Oh well. Go ahead and preheat now anyway and it'll be perfectly warm by the time you've done with steps 1-3.)

1. Brown the butter. All of it. But seriously, slightly caramelized butter is a game-changer. Need I say it again? BROWN THE BUTTER.

2. Using an immersion blender OR the power of your wrist (mine got jacked up in a motorcycle accident so I use the power of robots), mix together the deliciously browned butter, sugars (ALL OF THE SUGARS!), eggs, vanilla, and SECRET INGREDIENT aka almond extract for like 2 minutes or something.

3. Add in the flour, baking soda, and salt until it's barely combined, and then stir in the chopped up chunks of baking chocolate. The irregularity of the chopped up chunks is key to max delish. Seriously, you'll thank me later.

4. Divide up the dough into little balls of deliciousness. Bake about 9-11 minutes depending on how done you like your cookies. Or look: skip this step and just eat the dough. I won't judge you, but I also hereby absolve myself of any responsibility if you get salmonella poisoning. It's unlikely, though, and cookie dough is a well-known cure for most problems so...

*You can pry my cute little bee themed American measuring cups from my cold, dead hands.

The Building Blocks of a Marriage

Tiny, everyday moments are the building blocks of life—and of a marriage.

I would measure a successful marriage by how often one feels contented, supported, cared for, considered, and understood. Some of these feelings are so small they may be overlooked—when was the last time you truly enjoyed the feeling of contentment?[16]

This is in direct opposition to how most Westerners are typically raised. We watch Disney movies and see only the heart-melting love story: we don't see what happens when, after a decade of only vacationing on a tiny island in the middle of the ocean to be closer to Ariel's family, Eric snaps and books two weeks in the Moab desert or Ariel has a midlife crisis when she realizes how freaking awesome it was to have fins and she gave it up for what? An idiot prince who didn't even realize that some imposter wasn't her?? We read romance novels which follow extremely prescriptive patterns and generally have a guaranteed HEA—romance-novel lingo for the Happily Ever After.

We are taught to look at the big picture: The end justifies the means.

Now, I have no beef with either Disney or romance novels generally speaking,[17] but we are taught to see them as road maps for real life in a way that is pretty unhealthy. As long as we're getting that ring, that walk down the aisle, that nod of approval from our families and society at large... it's all worth it. Right?

In short: we're often taught that the value is in the wedding, not the marriage.

This is why we find so many individuals in unhappy relationships—the red flags that they almost certainly felt on a daily basis were not deemed important enough to get in the way of Relationship Success. Red flags like having mismatched sex drives, or different ideas about what's fun to do on a Friday night, or drastically different concepts of what a "clean" bathroom looks like. We absorb through cultural osmosis that these are trivial, superficial problems secondary to the overall goal of being married.

But unless you're actually living Groundhog Day (in which case you have serious problems out of my scope to handle), **your daily life does not consist of your wedding day over and over and over.**

It's made up of the grimy bathroom you have to use multiple times a day. Of deciding that playing co-op video games until the wee hours of Saturday morning is a perfectly reasonable grown-up activity. Of realizing your libidos aren't in sync, and having real discussions about solutions for that instead of simply ignoring it because giving up your sex life is inevitable in the confines of a marriage (it's not).

These little things become particularly important for expat couples, because it's so easy to get caught up in the pomp and circumstance of an international or intercultural relationship, especially if long-distance happens to be or have been a part of your particular story.

When you're busy planning your next trip or navigating a language barrier, it's easy to forget to show an interest in the books your spouse loves to read. When you've moved house three times in the last year, it's easy to forget about the fact that your partner has literally never taken out the trash. When you live in a country known for its opera, it's easy to forget that your spouse loves the blues and hasn't seen a performance in years.

It's easy to forget the little things—until it isn't.

THE BUILDING BLOCKS OF MARRIAGE

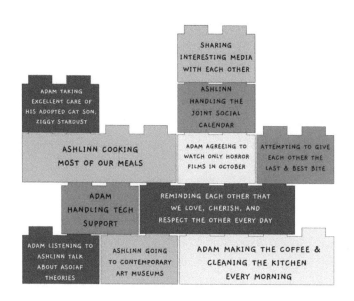

SHARING INTERESTING MEDIA WITH EACH OTHER

ADAM TAKING EXCELLENT CARE OF HIS ADOPTED CAT SON, ZIGGY STARDUST

ASHLINN HANDLING THE JOINT SOCIAL CALENDAR

ASHLINN COOKING MOST OF OUR MEALS

ADAM AGREEING TO WATCH ONLY HORROR FILMS IN OCTOBER

ATTEMPTING TO GIVE EACH OTHER THE LAST & BEST BITE

ADAM HANDLING TECH SUPPORT

REMINDING EACH OTHER THAT WE LOVE, CHERISH, AND RESPECT THE OTHER EVERY DAY

ADAM LISTENING TO ASHLINN TALK ABOUT ASOIAF THEORIES

ASHLINN GOING TO CONTEMPORARY ART MUSEUMS

ADAM MAKING THE COFFEE & CLEANING THE KITCHEN EVERY MORNING

Avoid the Sunk Cost Fallacy

It is a rare person who has not fallen prey to the sunk cost fallacy at one point or another. If you've never heard that phrase before, allow me to explain: a sunk cost is money or effort or anything of value, really, that has already been spent and is irretrievably lost. Like Rose's necklace, the *Heart of the Ocean*, at the end of *Titanic*.[18] A fallacy is a false or mistaken idea, or an argument that *seems* reasonable but isn't.

Combine the two, and you have a situation where you continue to invest in something—say, a toxic relationship—simply because you have already invested a great deal into it—say, thousands of the currency of your choice to move overseas or a decade of your life or a promotion to relocate to be near your partner. The idea is that since you've already put so much in, you may as well keep going. In for a penny, in for a pound, right?

NO. No! That's why this is a fallacy. It sounds almost reasonable, but it isn't. *You are never going to get your initial investment back, and continuing to drop priceless artifacts into the sea is the actual definition of madness.* I mean, Rose letting go of the *Heart of the*

Ocean was a metaphor for finally moving on from Jack, etc. etc., and we two art-loving members of the La Coppia Utopia household of course make allowances for the artistry of filmmaking. But that doesn't mean that *you* should go tossing your treasures into the sea.

I hear people complaining all the time about rising divorce rates, and while yes, it's true that one of the cutest, most moving sights in the world is an ancient couple tottering on the wedding dance floor alone because they're the only ones in the room who were married before Neil Armstrong flubbed his moon landing line... again, that's *one moment* in a sea of others.

Longevity in a relationship is not proof of quality. I genuinely hope that all of those old couples are truly happy. I hope she eagerly looks forward to coming home to him after a three week trip to Thailand with her senior girlfriends and he does the dishes every night with a bottle of red wine while she relaxes.[19] But the fact is, many of our forebears didn't have the kind of options and choices that many of us do today in whom to marry, when to marry, or *whether* to marry. Particularly women. And for so many, once you tied the knot? It was marriage until death, with divorce either completely illegal (as it still is in some countries) or at the very least so frowned upon socially that it was functionally not an option (and still isn't, in some religions and cultures).

It's not actually that hard to make it to that cute wedding shuffle if you a) managed to live long enough to see the day and b) had no other choice.

Happily, for many people around the world—though certainly

not all—there are now more choices available. If we're *not* happy, we can choose to leave.

The trick is knowing when to stay and do the work to try to fix something you care about and when to cut your losses and skedaddle with whatever you haven't sunk into the relationship—even if it means leaving behind the precious things you've already given up.

For expats this can be exceptionally difficult, because we've often been asked to put *so much* at risk before the relationship has had a chance to really take root. Here are a few common ones:

You've Overcome Cultural Barriers

In this instance, you've already done so, so much work on understanding your partner and the culture they come from. Maybe you've finally gotten your partner to try therapy or even gone toe to toe with an overbearing mamma. Did you finally stand up to her for nothing??

You've Overcome Logistical Barriers

Honestly, what we went through getting Adam's carta di soggiorno (a permit to stay for spouses of Italians) almost felt more monumental than March 2020, which is saying something because, if you remember, for us that month included a tornado destroying my house, surgery, the loss of a job, and of course, the COVID-19 pandemic lockdown. I can understand if you feel like you want to give a relationship another chance because you've spent *just that many hours* at the local police station or on the phone with a lawyer in a foreign language.

You've Survived Long-Distance

Long-distance is *hard*. Even nowadays, when you whipper-snappers have all of the new fangled apps and video calls and stuff. Back in my day,[20] we had to use the demo version of Skype that inevitably ran out of credit mid–extremely heartwrenching call—at best. At worst, we had to pay extortionate amounts to use *landlines* amidst nosy college roommates who wouldn't leave even for your insufficient 15 minutes of whispered nothings with your love. But while apps are fun, they simply aren't in-person hangouts. Long distance requires a massive amount of dedication, drive, and emotional bandwidth, and thanks to our collective worship of the Power of Love we can become quite stubborn in wanting to be one of the Couples Who Made It.

The thing that many people don't think about, though, is that a long-distance relationship is not dissimilar from the leap off a skyscraper. To paraphrase Douglas Adams, it's not always the fall that kills you (though it can be), it's the sudden stop. In the context of an LDR, the killing stop often comes when you're no longer long-distance. You've put in all of that hard, hard work only to realize that the relationship is *still* hard work even without the distance (as all relationships are). Maybe you're not very happy, but after all you went through to keep the LDR alive, it usually feels worth one... more... try...

You Had to Leap Too Soon, You Regret It, and You're Ashamed

If you've ever asked the question "why did I/they do that?," the answer is probably *shame*. Even if you think it's because of fear or anger... it's probably secretly shame. Really, it seems to be the scary monster under the bed of the rest of our feelings, the one that drives the rest. Being in an expat relationship can mean making choices quicker than when you're in other relationships, even ones with an angry shotgun-bearing relative lurking menacingly in the background. Maybe you made some rash choices, and now you're too embarrassed to give up.

These are all completely understandable ways to feel about saving a relationship that's floundering. *But how can you tell when you're falling prey to the sunk cost fallacy and when you should leave?*

I'm sorry to say that there really is no way that anyone else can answer those questions for you. Each person has their own level of comfort with what they put into any project, romantic relationship or otherwise, and each person has their own understanding of when enough is enough.

However, knowing the sunk cost fallacy trap is out there is half the battle! And there are a few things you can do if you find yourself questioning your relationship.

1. As much as possible, decide for yourself what you're willing to sacrifice to be with your significant other *before* you're asked to do so. Would you move? Would you live with their parents? Would you go vegan? Would you agree to a long-term committed partnership, but not marriage? Would you forgo having children? Be honest with yourself—no one else has to know your truths, so you might as well be.

2. Figure out what your true deal-breakers are. Ending a relationship is hard—they are rarely so unequivocally terrible that the choice to leave is obvious. So if you *know* your deal-breakers and make a promise to yourself that they are triggers for your departure, you can stand by that—even if there are other things tempting you to stay. Try to imagine yourself separate from your current person or situation—

and if you find yourself making excuses or exceptions because of the person you love, reread the unconditional love essay earlier in Part I and recognize that you might be compromising more than you should. Just remember: admitting you feel a certain way to yourself doesn't have to mean you take action. It just means you're being honest with yourself, and that is never ever a bad thing.

3. Talk to trusted friends and family and really listen to what they have to say. Ultimately, you are the only one who really knows how you feel and what is truly going on in your relationship, but you'd be surprised how many informative and helpful perspectives you can get from others. Not only is hindsight twenty-twenty, but so is the view through binoculars.

The Sunk Cost Fallacy is a tricky one to navigate, and one of the most challenging things about it is that it is deceptively self-perpetuating—when you look back, you might realize a moment that would have been ideal to leave... *but that was six months ago and you've just moved cities together and bought a house, so now* would *absolutely be the wrong time.* Try to recognize these kinds of thought patterns in yourself and remember... there is almost never a *good* time to leave. Or, my preferred version of that... there is never a better time to get off a sinking ship than *right now.*

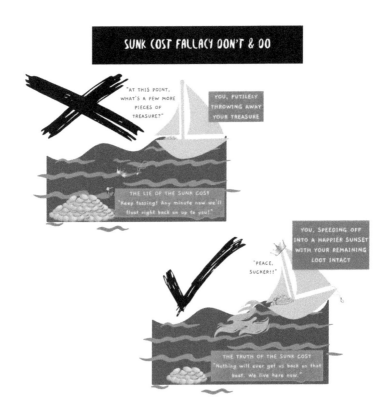

When "But That's How We Do It in My Culture" Is Just Another Way to Say "I'm an Asshole"

I have a conundrum for you that expats will find distressingly familiar: when are cultural norms curious differences to be understood and accommodated and when are they excuses for being an asshole?

We're all human and we have many commonalities as a species, but like it or not, different cultures have different values, practices, and ways of gauging what kind of behavior is acceptable and desirable.

A few European stereotypes: The Dutch are blunt. The Germans value orderliness above all. The French are open cheaters, whereas the Italians are secret cheaters.[21] These are shorthand stereotypes that mostly find their place as punchlines to jokes, but they grew out of observations of general cultural nuances.

Note that I said *general*. Not every person you encounter from a culture will have even a hint of that culture's stereotypes.

But the point is that cultures *are* distinctive, and learning the idiosyncrasies of a new culture is half the fun of dating someone in it! As anyone who has spent time in a foreign country will tell you, cultural differences are very real. I will never, never understand the Dutch obsession with leopard print any more than I will never fail to laugh at a video of an Italian person crying when they see someone add cream to carbonara.[22]

The problem comes when a partner does something that might infringe upon—or pole vault over—your boundaries, but dismisses your concerns or hurt feelings by chalking it up to a cultural difference.

Sometimes, this is fair enough. There are expectations and traditions in different countries that might feel incredibly foreign or bizarre at first, but whcih an outsider might find they can adapt to or even enjoy. I now kinda love that all of our shops in Italy are closed in August, for example—it's inconvenient, but brings me joy to think that pretty much everyone in my city gets to have, if not a vacation, a *break*, and that's an expected and normal thing. Or perhaps the issue we're talking about is something really small, like how you set the table or whether or not you can have a cappuccino *and* a Bloody Mary at brunch.[23]

More troubling are the times when I comfort a friend who is navigating a relationship where their partner isn't, for example, emotionally available, and is consistently unwilling to have conversations about the state of the relationship. Another common issue I see is one partner thinking that it's not their place to lift a finger to help in the home with chores. Unfortunately, these are often gendered problems, with my female friends somehow managing their careers, households, and family's social lives all at once.

I have heard all of these circumstances brushed off as "cultural differences." And that's not untrue, exactly. Historically, women have been expected to take care of the domestic sphere and patriarchal roots have had a huge effect on how many cultures manifest today. Beyond this, there are plenty of land mines to navigate when two or more different cultures collide: what role religion plays in daily life, how to celebrate holidays, how to educate and raise children, etc., etc.

And frankly, when a problem seems like it might be born of a culture clash, it can feel really challenging for the hurt partner to push back, asking themselves things like:

My partner says it's just a cultural difference. How could I, an outsider, know if that's true or not?

I knew the culture when I met my spouse. How can I expect them to behave any differently?

How can I ask my partner to change into something different from how they were raised?

As you can see, this subject becomes a maelstrom of anxiety, guilt, and hurt feelings.

In these instances, I recommend taking a step back.

At the end of the day, culture can explain *why* we do certain things, but it doesn't dictate our behavior: our actions are choices we make. I, for example, *choose* to force all of my foreign friends into Halloween costumes if they want to come to our annual party. I could be more lenient and let them simply show up and eat pumpkin pie and share my culture that way, but alas, I am a cruel and unyielding host.

I don't get upset if they choose not to come. I do roll my eyes, but ultimately their actions are their choices, just like mine are.

When you're in a partnership, you've made some implicit or explicit promises to value and care for your partner's well-being. If you do something that hurts your partner, that should matter to you—whether or not their feelings are, in your estimation, reasonable. The very least each partner can do is to *care* that the feelings have been hurt before diving into the whys and wherefores of the hurting.

At the end of the day, it doesn't really matter what cultural norms are; what matters is how you and your partner each feel within the context of the specific relationship that you are tending. If something you are doing repeatedly hurts your partner, it's time to put on your big boy skirt and *have a conversation about it.*

A conversation about the nuances of your relationship needs to be focused on just that: the two of you and your relationship. Ultimately, it actually doesn't matter what is accepted as reasonable within the context of a culture—what matters is whether *you* can accept it as reasonable within the context of *this* relationship.

Some people like spending every Sunday afternoon at their in-laws' house, some don't. Some couples are super physically affectionate even in public, some find that inappropriate. Some people not only don't care about infidelity, they actually get off on it. *That's all okay, as long as both parties genuinely agree to the arrangement.*

Why people behave in a certain way—because of cultural background, because of a childhood bully, because of a poem they read when they were on an ayahuasca trip in college—is fascinating for the purposes of understanding each other better, but it's actually secondary when determining whether actual lived behavior in a relationship is appropriate or not. It's good context to take into account, but not something to focus on.

I made a flowchart for dealing with pretty much any type of repeated offensive behavior, regardless of its origin:

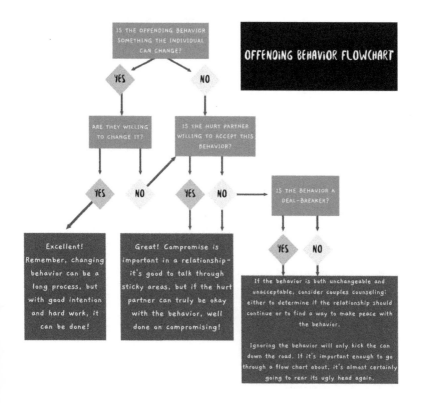

OFFENDING BEHAVIOR FLOWCHART

IS THE OFFENDING BEHAVIOR SOMETHING THE INDIVIDUAL CAN CHANGE?

YES — ARE THEY WILLING TO CHANGE IT?
NO — IS THE HURT PARTNER WILLING TO ACCEPT THIS BEHAVIOR?

YES — Excellent! Remember, changing behavior can be a long process, but with good intention and hard work, it can be done!

NO — Great! Compromise is important in a relationship—it's good to talk through sticky areas, but if the hurt partner can truly be okay with the behavior, well done on compromising!

YES — Great! Compromise is important in a relationship—it's good to talk through sticky areas, but if the hurt partner can truly be okay with the behavior, well done on compromising!

NO — IS THE BEHAVIOR A DEAL-BREAKER?

YES / NO

If the behavior is both unchangeable and unacceptable, consider couples counseling: either to determine if the relationship should continue or to find a way to make peace with the behavior.

Ignoring the behavior will only kick the can down the road. If it's important enough to go through a flow chart about, it's almost certainly going to rear its ugly head again.

For those of you listening to this without the benefit of seeing my snazzy flowchart, the order of operations for dealing with offensive behavior is:

1. Identify the offending behavior
2. Determine if this behavior is something the person can change
3. If it is, determine if they are willing to change it
4. If it isn't, determine if you're willing to put up with it
5. Determine if the behavior is a deal-breaker

If the offensive behavior is something they are willing to change, great! If not, but you can live with it—also great! Compromise is an important part of any relationship.

But if the behavior is both unchangeable and unacceptable, you need to consider couples counseling or some other way to give this behavior the attention it deserves. Ignoring hurtful behavior is only going to kick the can down the road. If it's important enough to go through a flow chart or read a book about, it's almost certainly going to rear its ugly head again in the future.

There are undoubtedly things about both of you that the other will find less than ideal. It's human nature—remember, we don't get to build our sandwiches to order. If a behavior is a deal breaker, it's a deal breaker and all other considerations fall away.

As someone much cleverer than I once said: just because there's only a tiny dollop of shit in your soup doesn't mean you should keep eating it for lunch. Deal breakers are like that: they ruin the pot. If they don't, they aren't deal breakers, and you can try to find coping mechanisms.

No one else gets to tell you what your deal breakers are, not for any reason at all. Trust yourself.

On the flip side, it's important to recognize that culture truly is a really, *really* strong mold, one that can take a lot of time and effort to break. It is also true that many individuals may not want to do so, and you cannot make them. That's their choice.

But you should never, *ever* let someone treat you as less than you deserve to be treated "because it's their culture." You can respect a culture without letting it dictate the details of your own life.

Ultimately, culture can be a helpful and useful explanation, but it is *not an excuse*. If there is a serious problem that your partner can't or won't resolve, it may simply be the end of the line for this particular relationship, and that's okay.

"Respecting cultural differences" is simply not a sufficient reason to stay in a relationship that isn't healthy or serving your needs as an individual.

WHEN BAD BEHAVIOR DRESSES UP AS
"CULTURAL DIFFERENCES"

Understand that Everyone Sucks Somehow

Now that I've hopefully made it perfectly clear that someone's culture is never an appropriate excuse for shitty behavior, it's time to let you in on another secret: everyone is shitty somehow, whether it's because of their culture or not.

It is admirable to work to accommodate your partner's needs and desires, presuming that they are willing to do the same for you. But there are limits to our ability to change—at some point, we are who we are, and there's a limit to how much you can change that. And you certainly cannot make someone else be someone they are not. No person is perfect. There are inevitably parts of each of us that aren't ideal, but also are kinda just part of the package.

This is how I ended up yelling "THIS IS HOW I SUCK" at Adam once during an argument fairly early on in our relationship, and I now think it's a great way to come to a better understanding of each other. Not the yelling, of course—the discussion of what pieces of ourselves are simply the frustratingly imperfect, all-too-human qualities.

I'm not really a yeller by nature, actually. In fact, sort of the opposite. When Adam and I met, I was a slow, simmering stone-waller. Which actually is a *massive* problem in relationships. Shutting down and not communicating is decidedly Not Help-ful, particularly when you're dating someone *very* emotional, as Adam is. He needs consistent discussion of feelings.

I was fully aware of *why* I had become a stonewaller. My relationship preceding Adam had been my only relationship that I look back on with disgust and horror.[24] It was emotionally abusive and traumatic. Nothing I said in the context of that relationship was taken for anything but what my ex wanted it to mean, and when you get snapped at or willfully misconstrued enough times, you eventually simply stop saying anything at all beyond the bare minimum in order to protect yourself.

So, like those who use culture as an excuse for their quirky behavior, I actually had a pretty understandable reason for being how I was. Unfortunately, having a sympathetic reason for being a stonewaller didn't change the fact that, well, I was shutting Adam out. Regardless of the *why*, I was still behaving in a way that was harmful to my current and much healthier relationship, and it needed to change.

So I Did My Own Work (more on that later). I worked on the stonewalling thing with a counselor and read a metric ton of books about it, which is my go-to method of figuring shit out. I wrote deeply personal essays about it. And, slowly but surely, I changed.

I became much more comfortable with vulnerability and openness. I learned to trust that Adam wasn't my ex and wasn't going to be abusive. I started to communicate effectively with

Adam when we were arguing, even if that communication was as simple as, "I love you and I'm not going anywhere, but I need some time to process this before I respond."

What I *didn't* do, despite my newfound ability to communicate feelings, was become extremely emotive. I didn't start gushing or engage in heightened and impassioned arguments (Adam's vibe).

That's how we came to the This Is How I Suck argument.

Some time after I'd done all of this work and made great progress, we got into an argument about something; I have no idea what. But at one point in this intense discussion, Adam pushed me pretty hard. He told me I was shutting him out emotionally, which I just *knew* in my gut simply wasn't the case. I just wasn't behaving as he did.

So I took a deep breath and just yelled, "THIS IS HOW I SUCK."

What I meant by that, and what I went on to explain to him after I took a breath, was that I'd heard his concerns about my stonewalling and had worked on it as hard as I could. He'd been right, after all: much as I'd hated to admit it, my emotional stonewalling—which to me just felt like being *safe*—would have eventually harmed or even destroyed our relationship.

But the fact remained that I simply was not—and never will be—a particularly emotive person. This still isn't even really a *bad* thing from my perspective: Maybe I don't share my deepest and darkest emotions[25] easily, but I also pretty much never say anything I don't mean—no thoughtless insults hurled to provoke a reaction, no angry words I later regret. I like that about myself, and so I will never be a no-holds-barred emoter.

At some point after I'd done everything I could to get rid of the unhealthy parts of my communication style, I'd reached my limit of change. I wasn't stonewalling anymore, but I also wasn't going to start suddenly expressing myself just like he did. Not being as emotive as him is, for Adam, one of the less-than-ideal ingredients in my sandwich.[26]

And so, it was up to him to decide if he could take me for the person I am, if the healthiest version of my way of disagreeing could work with his. That was how I sucked (for him).

We all suck in some way or another. The way you suck might have something to do with the family you grew up with or the culture you were raised in—it doesn't matter. What matters is to make good faith efforts to fix the broken parts so your metaphorical car is running smoothly. At the end of the day, self-improvement doesn't turn a Fiat 500 into a Jeep Renegade—it just makes sure that the vehicle is operating to the best of its ability.

And then it's up to your partner to decide if it's a car they can live with.

The Fifth Horseperson of the Expat Relationship Apocalypse

The Gottman Institute coined the concept of the Four Horsemen which consists of the following: Criticism, Contempt, Defensiveness, and Stonewalling. If you're curious about what these four features have in common, it's this: they feature in pretty much every ruined wreck of a relationship, either separately or as one relentless, unyielding coalition of doom.

For expats, I would unequivocally add *resentment* to this formidable list.

I have never seen resentment lead anywhere good, other than the kind of really indulgent sulk that *feels* good but actually drains your soul.

Its harbingers are Bitterness and Regret, and they are equally unwelcome to the party, but at least their presence can warn you that Resentment is on the way over with a six pack of Four Loko,[27] some lighter fluid, and a match. You can try to text it the wrong address or maybe just abandon your house altogether, but either way I think we can all agree: *resentment is not a guest you want to entertain.*

I am sorry to say that I have seen resentment figure very heavily in expat relationships. I've said it before and I'll say it again, but the fact is that when multiple cultures and countries are involved in a romance, it forces some tough choices to be made, often when relationships (or their constituents, or both!) are relatively young. That is resentment's perfect breeding ground.

In the throes of love, we don't always look ahead to the consequences of romantic choices: the career that might be sacrificed, the languages lost, the travels cut short, the home base set up somewhere we'd never before imagined.

Changing your life plan isn't inherently bad in and of itself. We all do it regularly, and good thing, too—I wouldn't want to be chained to the hair color(s) I chose when I was in my teens and early twenties, much less a partner or a career.

I, for example, was always a proudly independent hard worker. In fact, one time, when little Ashlinn was asked what I wanted to be when I grew up, I answered, "A workaholic! And maybe I'll get married when I'm thirty." At the time, of course, thirty seemed as distant from my tender age as Kepler-22b (a planet in the habitable zone of its star!) is from Earth. Someplace potentially recognizable, but impossibly far and difficult to imagine.

When Adam and I were deciding where to start our lives as a married couple, I realized that if we wanted to live abroad I would probably have to sacrifice my career in project management, at least for a while. This was not an easy proposition to swallow: after almost a decade in New York City and then

Nashville working with some of the most high profile clients in the world, I was both in demand and really good at my job. Plus, who would I even be if I wasn't a workaholic?

The decision was *not* easy, but it had to be made. Ultimately, the call of the road was stronger for me.

But I wasn't wrong about the consequences. For two years I didn't work in that industry at all, and I had no expectation of returning. I dealt with imposter syndrome, questions of identity, and a pathological need to be productive. More on that in a future Expat Career Guidebook. But I also got the opportunity to write more, work on creative projects, and *rest*.

Two years later, I actually did make my way back into the field, but in a much healthier, saner way with a better knowledge of who I am and *why* I work.

But even though in the end I haven't had to fully leave that particular career path behind, I had no way of knowing in advance that things would work out this way. I could never have predicted that COVID-19, a disease that had wrought so much pain and misery for so many— myself included—would also be instrumental in normalizing remote work, even for high profile agencies and clients.

These questions come up so frequently for expats as they navigate where they want to live and how. When we left the United States, I had to acknowledge the fact that I was walking away from a career I'd built through immense effort by surviving sleepless nights, painful meetings, and years of facing the pitiless grind that is New York City. I, an extremely independent person, also had to accept the fact that for a while, I was going to be financially dependent on my husband who worked in an industry I hadn't believed anyone *actually* made a living in before I met him. Seriously, there are real humans who actually pay their bill being *voice actors*?

I hadn't been *thrilled* about this, but it also had to happen for us to move. So we thought about it, talked about it, and made the best decision we could with all the information we had at the time.

It turned out just fine—far better than fine, in fact— but the truth is that none of us know the future. Leaving the US, where I had work connections, meant taking a huge gamble—a gamble that the chance to live abroad would be worth it, that I could return to the industry at a later date if it turned out to be a mistake, that I wouldn't sit on the couch day after day with Bitterness and Regret, just waiting for Resentment to slowly bubble up to suffocate our marriage.

You can't tell the future, either.[28] You will never, ever know for sure in the moment of decision if it's the right choice, the wrong one, or somewhere in between. All you can do is keep an eye out for Bitterness and Regret, and deal with those fuckers *before* Resentment can rear its ugly head.

Because by that point, it might be too late.

Do Your Own Work

It can be fun to look in the mirror. I like trying on new lipsticks, weird expressions, funky hairstyles! What is *not* fun is looking in the mirror when you *have* to. Like before a job interview or nerve-wracking date or because you have a weird growth you need to inspect.

Unfortunately, looking in the mirror when we don't necessarily want to do so is unavoidable in the modern world.[29] That's true both when you need to check out that runny mascara and it's true in the more metaphorical sense of looking deep into your own psyche and soul.

It's quite hard to overstate the importance of working on yourself, both for your own sake but also for the sake of your relationship.

As wonderful as our relationships are—both our intimate partnerships and our friendships—at the end of the day, we are our own closest companions. We have no choice but to live with our own thoughts, feelings, instincts, and inner narratives—in fact, according to Descartes, as far as we each know, we're the only things that actually exist, anyway.

I understand that this can feel a little frightening—I, too, would probably rather know for sure that Dolly Parton exists than myself—but I encourage you to see this situation for the gift that it is. If I walked into a room with two boxes, one labeled "ALMOST CERTAINLY NOTHING AT ALL BUT MAYBE A PIECE OF DECADENT TIRAMISU" and one labeled "DEFI-NITELY OREOS," I know which one I'd invest my time and energy into opening.

It sounds corny, but I have to say it: *You are the oreos.* You definitely exist and you're pretty damn good, even if you wist-fully wonder if the probably nonexistent tiramisu wouldn't be better. In your own head, you have your greatest ally, best friend, and mentor built into your very own brain, at least in potentia. Getting to that level of relationship can be a bit tricky, but it's worthwhile.

Alas, there is so little in life that we can actually change. We can't change what others do. We can't change how others react. We can't change what others feel—and in point of fact, we also can't change what *we* feel. But what we can change is our relationship to our own feelings, how we react, and what we do. It may take some effort, but it is possible to shift the landscape of your mind, and in that possibility is hope.

Cultivate that landscape—be mindful of what you put into it, how you nourish it, what patterns are already ingrained and how they can be altered to best benefit you. You can make those oreos as satisfying and decadent as any nonna-made tiramisu.

I'm sorry to say that nobody is perfect. No amount of therapy or self-work will make *you* perfect. And you don't even need to be approaching perfect in order to enter into a relationship—far from it. But knowing that the relationship will inevitably take work, isn't it better to start that project with the right tools in good working order?

The right tools, of course, being *you* and good working order being your physical and mental health and well-being.

Physical Health and Well-Being

Physical health and well-being is a tricky subject, because the definition of health can vary quite broadly depending on your personal goals, your genetic makeup, and of course, any physicality-related mental struggles you may be having. Body image issues are a serious and rampant problem in our society, and I cannot begin to address them the way they deserve in this short book.

However, I can share with you my personal approach to physical wellness (and body image). Beyond occasionally checking in with a doctor to make sure I'm not actively dying,[30] I regularly ask myself the following questions:

1. Do I eat reasonably healthfully? For me, that means eating primarily vegetables, limiting sugar, and following my body's lead on eating times. For you, it might be a more specific way of eating or, as in the case of some of my Italian friends, it might involve a required gelato every day of summer.

2. Can I engage in the physical activity I want to engage in? For me, this means getting at least 7-10k steps per day, running one or two 5ks per week, and being able to say yes if invited to engage in something outdoorsy with friends

(like hiking or skiing). Many of you will probably have a higher bar for this.

3. Does my partner still want to get it? ...I think this one is self-explanatory.

Mental Health and Well-Being

When it comes to mental health and well-being, I take a similar approach for gauging my relationship with that nebulous entity I call "me." I call it the Selfs Triangle, and it consists of three gauges for my inner life: self-awareness, self-esteem, and self-confidence.

Each one builds on the other two and are integral parts of having a healthy inner life. My simple definitions of each are as follows:

Self-awareness is conscious knowledge of my own mind and existence and how it affects the outside world.

Self-esteem is how I feel about my own mind and existence.

Self-confidence is how I feel about presenting my own mind and existence to others.

By diving into each of the Selfs, you'll be able to get a better understanding of how your mental landscape is looking. Some people are quite self-aware, but lack -esteem and -confidence. Others have -confidence in spades, but very little -esteem. I think we can all agree that the worst—or at least, most infuriating—people are those without any self-awareness, especially if they have the other two. Ugh.

Once you've taken stock of what you've got going under the hood, you can begin to work on making it as healthy as possible.

Generally, there are two ways to do this, which I'll dive into a little bit below.

Therapy

I know I don't know you, but you probably need therapy. Or if you don't need therapy, congratulations—you're in the 0.00002% of the human population, so you should go ahead and meet with a therapist to get your special award.[31]

My point is that to be human is to be flawed, to have problems that it's often not possible—or at least more difficult—to resolve alone. It is not uncommon to have issues with one or more parts of your Selfs Triangle at one point or another in your life.

I know, I know. Therapy seems to be every interfering busy-body's go-to answer to the slightest problem these days. Whatever happened to a good old-fashioned cramming your feelings down with food/alcohol/exercise and moving on with your life?

The problem is that so many people recommend therapy because, well, *it works.*

Unfortunately, therapy is a science, not a magic, so that means that you sometimes need to tweak the parameters of the experiment before it works. This means trying different methodologies, different therapists, or different timing to get the desired result. It can take time, money, and be extremely disheartening—especially if you wait to start trying it out until you're in crisis mode, which is unfortunately what people often do.

But therapy is less like a shot of espresso and more like actually getting a decent night's sleep for more than two nights in a row: it's a lot harder to arrange and builds up over time. Which is why I tried to trick everyone in the first paragraph into going to therapy; there are certainly people who don't *need* it as urgently as others, who can even live perfectly healthy lives without it, but there's pretty much no one who wouldn't benefit from it at all.

Hell, if I could afford it, I'd never let a week go by without therapy. An educated and trained human who has to listen to my problems and offer constructive advice? Shit, yeah!

Which brings me to my next point: affordability. Mental health isn't often covered by insurance—in most places I've lived, it certainly isn't—and it can often have a negative stigma attached to it. This makes it hard to find the appropriate resources, and it's not cheap. And it really shouldn't be, considering the aforementioned training of said therapists. They gotta eat, too.

So what do you do when a random person whose book you happened to pick up tells you you need therapy but you don't have the cash?

One option is to look into more affordable or less conventional options than traditional one-on-one talk therapy.

This might include the use of an app—of *course* there's an app for that—that connects you with a mental health specialist for a cheaper rate.

It might also look like signing up for group sessions of some sort, which can also be conducted over the internet. Every Tuesday night, Adam meets with a men's group where they talk about how great of a wife I am (I assume) while I play video games. It costs nothing but time and dedication.

This isn't really an ideal substitute for actual therapy sessions—and if you've experienced acute trauma, there truly isn't a substitute for it—but these other options can be very helpful, either because you've found a quality option that works for you or simply because you're taking the time and effort to invest in your mental health, even if it's not the perfect solution.

If even that is too expensive, too hard, or you hate group sharing—or perhaps you just aren't ready to take the dive into therapy (and that's okay, but I hope you'll get there some day)— keep reading.

Self Work

Self work is pretty much what it sounds like: work you do on yourself, alone, to help improve your Selfs Triangle.

There are pretty much limitless ways to do this, but here are some of the most common:

1. Consume pertinent media.

   I, personally, am a big book reader, but podcasts, movies, articles are all great ways of diving into your Selfs Triangle exploration. In the appendix of this book, Adam and I have both contributed to a list of resources—books, podcasts, movies—we have found helpful doing our own deep dives into the deep darkness that is our selves. Some of these are geared specifically for expats.

2. Practice meditation.

   A classic solution that really helps you work on that self-awareness point of the Selfs Triangle. This can include ohm-style sitting and thinking, guided meditations, or even yoga or other physical activities meant to tap into the thoughtful or spiritual side of life. Strangely, I find recording audiobooks quite meditative. Again, there are many apps for this. It just requires a little time and dedication to figure out what works best for you.

3. Follow a guided course.

By guided course, I mean workbooks or even lessons you can find that aim to take you through various practices to help you excavate deep down into your psyche.

4. Journaling.

You would think that, being a lover of the written word, I would be a big journaler, but the truth is, I'm not. I have managed to keep a word document going since March 15, 2020, but with only the most sporadic updates, sometimes with months and months between each entry. My point is, you don't have to be a journaler even if you like to write, and similarly, you don't have to be a writer to be a journaler. But a whole lot of people find writing, even just for ten minutes a day, incredibly helpful.

Read, Write, Run

A long time ago, I codified my approach to both mental and physical health. As you can probably tell by now, I like easy-to-recall, self-explanatory statements that way oversimplify matters.

I call it, not particularly creatively, Read, Write, Run, or RWR for short.

It's actually that simple.

Every day, I aim to do two (I'm only human) of these three things:

Read - Bring something valuable from the external world into my consciousness.

Write - Put something of my own into the world.

Run - Do something for my physical health and wellness.

Your version of this might be Listen, Paint, Rock-Climb, or Smell Flowers, Cook, Jazzercise. It doesn't really matter.

The idea is to do at least two things per day that help your mind and body to get the exercise they need, no matter how small. The reason for only doing two of these things is to set a reasonable goal since some days you may just not have the attention span to read or the inclination to run. Frankly, with work and socializing and being married and learning Italian and and and... I often just don't have *time* for more than two of those.

I codified this credo when I was going through a rough patch several years ago, because no matter how disgusted or angry I was with myself, no matter how much of a failure I felt—and damn, did I feel like a failure some days—I couldn't help but acknowledge (however grudgingly) that I wasn't all *that* bad if I had managed to do at least one of those useful things that day.

And the best (possibly most satisfying) part? My handy little tools—the Selfs Triangle and RWR—work perfectly together.

It's hard not to be self-aware if you're mindfully RWRing every day.

It's hard not to have some self-esteem if you've accomplished a goal you've put to yourself, like RWR.

And it's hard not to gain some self-confidence if you have some self-esteem.

Thus, the cycle feeds itself.

A Final Note on Doing Your Own Work

Please don't get me wrong in this section: I'm not saying that you have to be in perfect, tip- top mental health and love every second you spend trapped in your own mind in order to be in a relationship.

There *are* some schools of thought that say that you must love yourself before anyone else can love you, but they are pretty outdated and lean very heavily into the kind of toxic positivity that prevents people from being truly honest with themselves—a prerequisite for real healing.

I would probably amend that to "you should be open to loving yourself and actively working towards it before you should con- sider engaging in a romantic relationship with another person, or at least be *very, very careful* when doing so."

Incidentally, that's why I'm not a famous writer yet. Not enough pithy one-liners. Nobody ever put a quote like that one on an instagram square.

The fact is that you're never going to be in perfect tip-top mental health and love every second you spend trapped in your own mind. You're human, like me: we don't get that luxury. You certainly can, should, and really *must* continue working on your- self even after you find your dreamiest dream partner.

But beyond the benefits you inherently receive for yourself by working on your mental and physical health and well-being, you want to be in the best position possible for your dreamy partner whenever they do find their way into your life.

Chances are you're going to be better positioned for a healthy relationship if you've already done some reconciling within your- self—and chances lessen that you might do harm to a person that you are growing to care about. Be a responsible potential partner, and start working on your shit!

Plus, all that work on yourself is going to come in handy for the *next* section...

A PiCTURE OF THE KiND OF PEOPLE WHO COULD BENEFiT FROM THERAPY

Okay, this one would have been more effective if I had the budget to include a reflective surface.

Do Your Together Work

"It's like having a referee," my friend said to me one sweet-scented summer evening in Nashville. We were talking about our relationships, a favorite subject, and she'd just shared that she and her husband had spent considerable time in couples counseling.

Couples counseling.

I can't think of many other two-word phrases that can strike such a particular combination of fear, anxiety, disgust, and despair into the heart. If the judgment on individual therapy is pretty severe, judgment on couples counseling is astronomical, and not the pretty stars kind of astronomy. The black hole kind of astronomy. The destructive kind.

I'd say that, generally speaking, most people presume that if you're in couples counseling it's all but a death warrant for your relationship. It clearly means things are truly awful and you're in the trenches ready to waste hundreds or thousands of dollars on some therapist who is only going to tell you what you already know: DTMFA.[32] So why waste the time?

The truth is that counseling gets a bad rap because it often can lead to breakups. I think this is because a lot of couples wait until their relationship is already on life support before even entertaining the concept of going to see a counselor. That's kinda like waiting for gangrene to set in when you could have gotten the cut stitched up when it was small.

Another truth is that **couples who work mindfully through their problems with the help of a professional can come through all kinds of problems—even infidelity, even cultural clashes— much stronger for it.**

It's a little wild to me that of all of the important roles we can potentially play in life, the ones with the most impact on others—like being a partner, a parent, or a plumber—only the last one requires actual classes and training to accomplish. We're not really ever *taught* to be a good spouse, we're just sort of supposed to absorb it through osmosis or through fumbling and awkward attempts at dating when we're teens.

Imagine if you went to hire a plumber to fix your toilet and he said, "Don't worry, I took a lot of craps in high school. I know what I'm doing!"

Back to my friend, whose single sentence probably had more of an effect on my marriage than any other single external influence. Having a couples counselor was like *having a referee.*

And just like that, my entire conception of couples counseling—what it was for, but even more than thatso, what it *could* be used for—shifted, and I found myself hatching a pretty wild idea. What if Adam and I went to see a couples counselor *before we even had any problems?* What if we got used to the idea of talking to someone and gave them the opportunity to get to know us while we were in a good phase of the relationship?

I broached the subject carefully with Adam. We had been

dating for about six really lovely months at this point: We'd said our I love you's and had some preliminary discussions about that we were both of us hoping that the relationship would work out. We'd already had our first argument and we knew there were certain things that needed working on (in a nutshell, because I know you're curious, my lack of emotional expression and his overwhelming emotional expression).

So why the hell wouldn't we consider connecting with a professional about it? We could afford it and it would only really cost time and an open mind. I pitched the idea to Adam and he was, happily, very game to give it a try.

You see, we had both had experiences with couples counseling in the past, albeit largely for relationships that were absolutely in the gangrene/life- support stage. But despite the those outcomes of those situations, we'd overwhelmingly had good experiences with good counselors. Mine had done a phenomenal job at helping me safely extricate myself from a very bad situation. Adam had a positive experience with a counselor helping him and his first wife restructure their relationship about a year before they ultimately decided to end their marriage.

Once we started thinking about it, it was sort of *exciting*, and it just plain made sense. *All* relationships, in our collective experience, eventually faced immense challenges of some sort. What if we started going to a couple's counselor *before* those problems arose, so the counselor would have some knowledge of us ahead of time? That way, there'd be no need to waste time on background context when we had a sticky situation to navigate: we could dive right on into the muck. We were going to be the most prepared couple *ever*. We were going to *make sure this thing worked.*[33]

Believe it or not, that's precisely what happened. Our first meeting with David (our therapist) was lovely, and I'd pay money to know what he thought when we told him the plan, but he seemed pretty excited about it. I remember that he ended the session by asking us to look into each other's eyes for one minute, during which we dissolved into giddy smiles and love-sick giggles.

The next few sessions we talked to him about our personal histories and issues we were working on on our own (see above section). Then sure enough, a few sessions in, a specific issue arose around a specific argument, so we brought it to our session.

I'm happy to report that the system worked exactly as we'd hoped—exactly as my friend had said. David acted as a referee: He didn't get in the game, but he did slow us down and call us out on our bullshit when necessary.

At the end of the day, I don't think that we didn't get anywhere we couldn't have gotten on our own, but I *do* think that we did so with more speed and far less collateral damage than could have occurred without him.

After about four months, we stopped going to see him regularly, and thereafter simply engaged his services when a particular need arose. We'd laid the groundwork, so were very prepared to keep steering our ship on our own. But if a particularly troublesome issue arose, we'd schedule a session or two, or even just use the concept of going to see him to try to work out what healthier versions of our conversations we could be having. He was our premarital counselor in the weeks leading up to our marriage, and later guided us through the early months of being newly wed expats during the second lockdown.

I've said before that it is mind-boggling when you realize that none of us (or very few of us) are actively prepared for healthy, mutually-supportive relationships, and I think it shows. It's got to be at least partly why the divorce rate is as high as it is, because so many people just dive in without previous training or preparation. Learning from experience is great, don't get me wrong—in fact, Adam almost didn't date me *because* I had never been divorced and he wasn't sure I'd have the right experience and skills[34]—and why not try something that might set you up for the best possible success?

Ultimately, many of us could benefit from adjusting what we assume is needed to give our relationships the best possible chance to survive, if not absolutely thrive. It's a cop out and misleading to claim that "love" should be enough. It's not. It takes hard work—and hiring an expert to show you what that kind of work looks like just makes plain old-fashioned *sense*.

I know how powerful the stigma against couples counseling is, particularly in certain cultures. Hell, it's even stigmatized in mine and Adam's own home cultures! I know how powerful the stigma is because, honestly, Adam and I didn't tell anyone about what we were doing until long after we'd done it. I suppose on some level I simply wanted proof of concept (look, we got married! look, we're happy!) but if I'm honest with myself, and I always try to be, part of it was absolutely a feeling of shame over what I thought others might think if they knew. I didn't want those looks, those expectations that we were in trouble or anything but madly in love.

I'm over that now. Both because I don't actually give a fuck what other people think about our relationship and also because I think this might be one of my most important pieces of advice.

I'm not saying everyone needs to go out and get a couples counselor tomorrow. Adam and I are kinda weirdos, I know. Preemptive counseling was amazing for us, maybe not so much for you. But it's a good gauge to understand how your partner communicates about relationships and what they're willing to do, particularly when different cultures are involved. It has been a slow, slow march toward acceptance of even the lightest concepts of therapy at all in many cultures, a problem strongly tied to toxic masculinity and patriarchal norms. While this is changing, the chance can be glacially slow.

Despite that, I think it is absolutely critical to get a sense of how your significant other feels about the concept of counseling, both couples and otherwise. If you're not already permanently entangled, I entreat you to *seriously consider* if you should join your life to someone who would refuse to go, even if their reasoning is because it's not a part of their culture. You don't know what the future holds. Would you marry someone who wouldn't hire a plumber even if every toilet in your house was irreparably stopped up? At the very, very least, gain an understanding what they're counterproposal would be. If not counseling, what steps would they take to work on the relationship?

And if you both are open to counseling, consider being open to going *before* you think you need·it, or at least before the relationship has coded and needs to undergo the shock of resuscitation (I know it's fun when doctors yell "CLEAR!" on TV, but this is not the experience you want for your relationship).

If you take away *one thing* from this chapter, I hope it's that choosing to get help isn't a reflection on how much you love your partner or a judgment on the value of your relationship.

It's just hiring a plumber who actually knows how to use a pipe wrench.

PART TWO: TACTICS

If Strategy helps you understand a healthy way to approach relationships from a long-term, zoomed-out perspective, Tactics is here to help you survive the nitty gritty of day to day expat married life. After all—that's what a relationship is, right? The little moments, be they good or bad or silly. Hopefully a decent amount of silly!

Unfortunately, being an expat can come with far more than its fair share of bad—or awkward, or challenging, or just plain *strange*—moments that need patience and creativity to resolve. Let's launch into some of the more tactical pieces of hard-won advice Adam and I have pulled together over the years.

Remember The Stranger
You Fell In Love With

Your partner started out as a stranger, and it is the great wonder and great tragedy of relationships that they eventually stopped being one.

The concept of a stranger is an interesting one, and not just because I spent a fortnight during my sociology master's attempting to decode Georg Simmel. If you live in a big city or travel frequently, you yourself are certainly no stranger (hah) to what I've dubbed The Stranger Spectrum, which puts strangers on a spectrum based largely on how much or how little charisma you feel that they exude.

THE STRANGER SPECTRUM

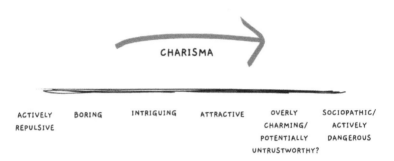

| ACTIVELY REPULSIVE | BORING | INTRIGUING | ATTRACTIVE | OVERLY CHARMING/ POTENTIALLY UNTRUSTWORTHY? | SOCIOPATHIC/ ACTIVELY DANGEROUS |

Most strangers one encounters have fairly minimal charisma; they generally hover roughly around the "boring" mark of the Stranger Spectrum, perhaps even veering into "repulsive" if you're aggressively introverted or they are just awful people. Strangers are the great unwashed masses, if we're being ungenerous. Or to put it plainly and less aggressively, most people are just... people.

As strangers move up the charisma scale from "boring" to "intriguing" or even "attractive," you'll find yourself becoming interested in turning these strangers into something else. It could be as simple as enjoying the exchange of a daily nod with the impeccably dressed older gentleman who does the crossword each morning in your coffee shop. He's intriguing! It could be as complex as meeting and getting to know the person you eventually marry. They're attractive!

Continuing up the scale through "attractive," we head into territories warranting a touch more caution. Have you ever met a person who was so thoroughly charming you weren't sure you could fully trust them? Yeah—exciting, but maybe not someone to invite into your inner circle. At the very extreme end of the scale are individuals who are sociopathic: those narcissistic charmers who worm their way into the apples of our lives only to leave us riddled with holes, if not completely inedible, by the time they're done.

I personally recommend looking for a partner or a spouse somewhere along the scale between intriguing and attractive, leaving the attractive-to-overly-charming crowd for sexy flings and completely avoiding the sociopaths. Unfortunately, they can be difficult to spot—a subject for its own book, but as always, listen to your gut if it's insisting that there are inconsistencies even though your eyes and heart are swooning. As a basic rule, you don't have to answer the question: Even just needing to ask yourself if someone is a sociopath is generally a bad sign and a massive red flag.

OPTIMAL ZONES FOR
PARTNER-SEEKING ON THE STRANGER SPECTRUM

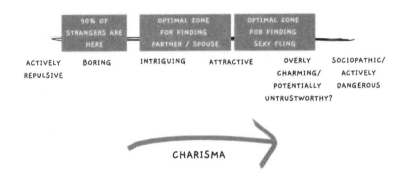

CHARISMA

For expats, it can take some time to decode cultural norms to understand how this scale works in different countries. For instance, the level of flirting exuded by individuals in some cultures might be perfectly normal within their own context but come across as "overly charming/potentially untrustworthy" in your home culture. This is why it's helpful to ask local friends for advice and take things slowly as you acclimate to a new culture and begin embarking upon adventures in dating.

So let's say you've found that person. Amazing! They're fascinating, appealing, engaging. Someone you want to know absolutely everything about to the point where you put a ring on it, or at least cohabitate.

The problem is that upon entering into a relationship, the

Stranger Spectrum undergoes a curious change. Time and familiarity begin to put weights on one end of the spectrum.

THE RISKS UPON MARRYING A STRANGER

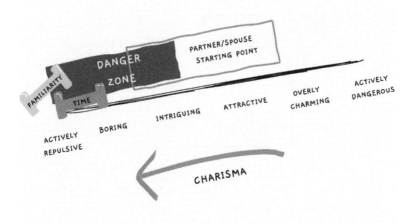

The point is that even the most exciting and sexy person can lose a bit of their shine after a while. This isn't news: plenty of studies talk about the slow dissipation of hormones that cause the so-called Honeymoon Period in relationships to end after a year or two, and the Seven Year Itch isn't just a great film starring Marilyn Monroe. And seriously, if the husband of a woman as smart and interesting[35] as *Marilyn Monroe* was starting to get bored, what hope do any of us have?

In truth, I'm happy to say that we have a lot of hope. However, as with anything in marriage, that hope is founded upon dedication and persistence with a single goal in mind.

The goal is this: **Remember the stranger you fell in love with every single day.**

It is so easy in the context of marriage to take each other for granted. One of the greatest strengths of marriage is knowing your partner will be there, for better or for worse—but this is also one of its greatest weaknesses.

It is easy, in the routine of everyday life, to forget that the person we've chosen to spend each day with is a creature of infinite nuance and depth, of dynamic and changing thoughts, opinions, and quirks.

And as expats, when there are *so many new things* to learn and experience in a foreign country, it can be easy to deprioritize the person you know the best. After all—with so many new words and customs to learn, so many new people to meet—time for reengaging with someone you already feel you know well feels scarce. Plus, any time you relocate, your whole routine gets thrown off as you adjust to new ways of living. And then before you know it, you've begun to completely take your partner for granted.

Adam and I figured out a way to combat this by accident early on in our relationship. When we started dating, we had pretty mismatched lives: he was a voice actor who didn't really hop in the booth until four or five p.m. and I worked in advertising, which pretty much meant I worked until at least that time, usually a bit later, with occasional midnight or later work calls to catch my clients in Japan at a reasonable hour.[36]

The saving grace for our relationship was a pot of coffee and my porch. Somehow, despite the insane hours and expectations of the advertising industry, no one really starts to work until like ten a.m., which meant that mornings ended up being the time Adam and I could reliably spend together. I'd just bought a cute little yellow house in East Nashville (the one that, around a year after the time I'm describing, would be ravaged by a tornado) and anyone who has been to the south of the US knows what buying a house there means if you're lucky: a porch.

My porch wasn't quite the grand, sweeping expanse of my dreams. In fact, if I'm honest, it was barely a porch—maybe more like a glorified stoop. But there was enough space for two little chairs, though we mostly just sat cuddled up next to each other on the top step.

Every morning, we'd make a pot of French press coffee and go out to sit on that porch together for anywhere from thirty to ninety minutes, depending on what time we managed to emerge from bed. We'd make the coffee, drink the coffee, and talk, talk, talk. We realized early on that this was a special time and gave it its own name—Porch Coffee, rather uncreatively, but it became a ritual that followed us to Adam's back deck when we stayed at his house.

We would talk about all kinds of things. Art, politics, religion, books we were reading, stories from our childhoods. Although silence is golden, talking has been a—or maybe *the*—foundation of our relationship.[37]

But it's actually not really the talking that matters here: we could have sat together in silence and had a similar outcome. I'm also not *just* suggesting the tried-and-true idea of date nights: At that time, we also used to set up monthly fancy date nights where we would get all dressed up and eat burgers at different dive bars, but those were special occasions.

Porch Coffee is magical because it is entirely *unspecial*. The spirit of it is a mundane, everyday occurrence that is entirely about *you* and how *you* choose to see your partner. Share a coffee, go for a walk, listen to a new album, tell each other a secret.

The point isn't to get your partner to entertain you or impress you. It is about ensuring that *you* remember to experience your partner as a distinct individual separate from who they are as your partner every single day. Your partner isn't just your spouse or other half: They are a stranger, too. A stranger that, at one point, you fell in love with.

It doesn't have to take long—it's a perspective shift that can happen in an instant or an hour. And it sounds overly simple, but finding your Porch Coffee and remembering the stranger you fell in love with is like getting your ten thousand steps a day or taking a multivitamin: something small that can make an incredible difference over time.

Make Your Peace With The Expat Tax

Adam and I have spent hundreds—maybe even thousands, *yikes!*—of dollars on what we've come to term "The Expat Tax."

The Expat Tax consists of money wasted for dumb reasons that would easily be avoidable by anyone who is not a pea-brained foreigner, from municipal fines for misreading a parking meter to delectable-looking-but-turns-out-impossible-to-cook-by-anyone-but-the-most-experienced-nonna ingredients bought on a whim at the grocery.

On one truly infuriating day, Adam and I were accosted by not one, but *two separate sets* of bus police—a real thing that exists in Italy—during the *same bus ride*. Not for failing to have a bus ticket, oh no.[38] No, these four suited and booted heroes of the municipal system were angry at us for having *too many* bus tickets... of the wrong type. You see, once I realized that the tabaccheria's opening hours were unpredictable at best, but non-existent at worst, anxiety demanded that I never risk being without a bus ticket. So I bought a dozen of them at once, figuring that they surely had a longer shelf life than your average lettuce.

Unfortunately, it turned out that our grumpy suburban to-bacconist had sold us—the two stranieri, foreigners, in our little suburban satellite of Turin—a dozen one way tickets to go *away* from the city center instead of into it.

The first set of bus police were begrudgingly understanding as I proudly held up my incorrectly-colored ticket. The second set? Not so much. I have detailed this encounter in painstaking detail elsewhere, but what ensued was a truly bizarre macho standoff between Adam, who couldn't *believe* that another set of bus police were harassing us about an innocent mistake, and an impeccably uniformed and unyielding young man who took a little too much pride in his position of relative authority.

This multi-lingual argument culminated in us being hauled off the bus and handed over to the *real* police (who looked positively incredulous that the bus tyrant was bothering them with something so trivial—I'd love to know more about the hier-archies among public servants here), with me trying to explain in frantic, broken Italian that *yes*, we realized our tickets were the wrong ones, but that the previous bus police had told us to simply finish our ride and get the right tickets next time.

The whole crew—bus police and real police alike—stared at the stack of tickets I was waving in their face and, to my great confusion, began arguing about the date when I'd bought them, among other things. The end result is that we ended up with a seventy Euro fine in addition to the twenty-ish euros I'd already spent on now-useless bus tickets.

The point is that **the Expat Tax is incurred when you don't**

necessarily do anything *wrong*, you are just out money (and, usually, time) because of language or cultural barriers that would
never have happened in your home country. That makes it feel
so *wasteful*, so silly. In the US, I'd never mistake a bus ticket
"from Turin" with one "to Turin."

These scenarios make me feel unbelievably foolish and throw
into sharp relief the strange waters we tread in foreign rivers.[39]
But the harsh reality is that living in a new country comes
with the deadly combination of operating in a foreign language
and often-unwritten or seemingly inconsistent rules. This will
naturally lead to inefficiencies and frustrations, occurrences that
lead one to forehead-smacking, sky-cursing, and, perhaps most
unfortunately, nonconsensual wallet-lightening, but all you can
do is make your peace with this fact of expat life.

Financial struggles are often a source of tension for any
couple—I can remember my mother telling me that money was
really the only thing she and my father ever fought about in
thirty happily married years. And for expat couples, this source
of anxiety can be even deeper, because no matter how you slice
it, it's *expensive* to move.

It's setting up a new household: There wasn't space in the
suitcase for your appliances (and maybe you'd have to buy a
converter for each one anyway) but damn if you don't need a
hand blender and a hair dryer. It's trying out new products at
the shop—is that laundry detergent *for* light clothes, or *to lighten*
clothes? *Oops!* It's spending more on eating and drinking out
than you would have normally because you're desperately trying
to make new friends.

Instead of getting bent out of shape over money that we

could have saved "if only we knew x, y, or z...," we decided to corral these instances into a specific category: the Expat Tax.

By naming and acknowledging this phenomenon, as a couple we a) made space for the undeniable fact that there were sometimes going to be sometimes costly learning curves living in a new place and b) found a way to commiserate *together* and shrug off any question of blame.

Because if money is tight, it's not hard to edge dangerously close to the line between "exasperation" and "resentment" when a partner brings home a parking ticket or a dozen beers that were on sale because, as it turns out, they were skunked and your partner didn't even think to look at the expiration date (or misread it because we list the day and month backwards in the US). These instances can feel frustrating or silly.

But the point of the Expat Tax is to remind you both that these mistakes *aren't silly.*

Navigating a new language and/or culture inevitably comes with errors, sometimes expensive ones.[40] And it's simply not worth spending time and energy agonizing over inevitable occurrences or beating yourself up over something that, in retrospect, seems obvious. You're not a bad person for being a little out of your depth and you're not a stupid person for misunderstanding something that you later realized should have been obvious. Life is never perfectly efficient, except maybe in Germany, so cut to the chase and forgive yourself.

Just as you might include an extra 120 euro in your budget one month because you needed new running shoes, go ahead and add whatever was spent to the tally of this month's Expat Tax and move on. Spend your time focusing on the important things, like laughing together over the bus police's absurdly starched and impeccably braided uniforms or how quickly the macho bus tyrant's tune changed from indignant rage to warm friendliness —once you'd forked over the fine.

After all, you will both contribute to the Expat Tax either together or separately at various points. The important thing is that you and your partner are in this *together*.

Do What You're Good At 80% of the Time

In those halcyon days of first living together, each partnership is faced with a harsh reality: There are things that your partner is better at than you. That's okay, though: You're better than your partner at other things.

Take Adam and me, for example. I am an objectively better cook than Adam, who in the years immediately before he met me subsisted exclusively on butter coffee, eggs and bacon, and something we now call sludge.[41] And beyond that, I actually *enjoy* cooking. The process relaxes me and puts me in a zen frame of mind I simply cannot achieve through meditation. Maybe it's the Italian blood speaking, but I just love food, both the eating and sharing of it. So I do the lioness's share[42] of the cooking.

Adam is much cleaner than I am. I try to tell myself that it's okay because I'm "untidy but not unclean," but the truth is that he wins on both counts. Plus, he loves doing the dishes, which is a great counterbalance to the whole me cooking thing.

Despite this, and despite the fact that Henry Ford proved beyond the shadow of a doubt that specialization is a waaaay more efficient way to make cars, we've found that it's essential that no one person perform the same exact tasks all the time, even if they are tasks they enjoy.[43]

Just because I like cooking doesn't mean I want to be responsible for the entire family's nutrition all the time. Just because Adam finds dishes-doing meditative and satisfying doesn't mean he doesn't smile with relief when he sees that I've taken care of them one afternoon.

A good practice for us has been to do the tasks that we are good at/like doing/have decided to take responsibility for 80 percent of the time. The other 20 percent of the time, the other partner is expected to pick up the slack. And that's not a prescriptive rule (not that anything in here is, you can literally just choose to ignore me). Your number might be 60 percent or 95 percent—*as long as it's not 100 percent.* It can even be 50 percent, though I'm still enough of a fan of efficiency that I think if someone is better at or enjoys a task, it's preferable to let them do it more often.

"But Ashlinn," I hear you saying, "then why not just take on cooking as your task and just ask Adam to take over dinner one night or another as needed? That's just good communication, right? And clearer. You like clarity!"

I'm so glad you asked. Yes, yes that IS good communication, and there's absolutely nothing wrong with asking your partner for help with a chore or task. BUT. You know what's *really* nice?

Not having to ask all of the time.

The 80 percent rule doesn't mean we literally split things up eighty-twenty, counting and measuring each plate scrubbed and glass rinsed. The point is that if a few days have gone by where I haven't even so much as glanced at the sink, I get a tingly little spidey sense that reminds me that it might be time to pick up a sponge. I only get that because I know that dishes, though not my primary chore, are partly my responsibility as a member of the household who dirties dishes.

Sure, 10 to 20 percent of the dishes isn't a ton, but it's kinda more about the nod to the shared bond that is the never-ending mountain of household tasks. Like when you pour a little beer out for your absent mates.

Beyond that, of course this will also vary depending on other factors in your life. Do you both work or not? Is childcare a factor? These are all elements that should be considered when figuring out how to divy up your life together.

And as for expats? Well, different cultures have very different expectations about who performs what tasks around the household. Many, unfortunately, still subscribe to patriarchal and outdated notions that women should take care of housework, or at the bare minimum be responsible for *managing* the household— invisible labor which is rarely actively factored into our understanding of individual or household productivity.

And sadly, there are even contingents of partners who claim that, well, of course they *would* help out more, but they simply *can't* do any of the chores. They don't know how!

I call bullshit on this. Nobody, barring actual disability, cannot perform the foundational parts of maintaining a household or relationship. When you or your partner say you or they *can't* do something, the problem is actually one of the following:

Actual problem: They don't *want* to do the chore.

Solution: Too bad for them. 80 percent rule stands. You can consider upping your contribution to 95 percent of the time, but they've still gotta do that 5 percent.

Actual problem: They don't do it the way you would do it/ you want them to do it.

Solution: Too bad for *you*. Adam washes the dishes *before* putting them in the dishwasher. It'll be a cold day in hell before I do that because a) it wastes water, b) it's completely unnecessary (in my opinion), and c) I'm "efficient" (read: lazy). There's nothing wrong with rinsing the crap off and then sticking the dishes into the dishwasher: as long as what they've done is effective and won't actively harm anyone (like only rinsing a cutting board that was used for slicing raw chicken or leaving chunks on the plates that could fuck up your dishwasher), the picky partner just needs to deal. It's *their* 20 percent.

Actual problem: They actually, truly don't know how to do it.

Solution: Sometimes, if I don't feel like sludge or breakfast for dinner, I'll take the opportunity to teach Adam how to make a simple meal, like soup or tomato sauce. We learn by being taught and doing things repeatedly. No, I'm not fully avoiding making dinner, but I do feel supported and like he's taking part when we do this. Plus, it's an investment in our future: next time, he *can* make it. I may still be doing the work, but I'm not fully responsible, which is sort of the point.

I have one other trick up my sleeve for when neither of you wants to do something: OTA. Which stands for "Order Takeout, Asshole," a particularly fun phrase to use when someone claims they can't cook to try to weasel out of dinner, but really can be used in many comparable situations. You see, pretty much every "I can't/don't know how to..." is just an excuse as it has some kind of simple solution or lifehack to address it. Can't change your oil? Look it up on YouTube, genius! Can't hang the TV? Hire a professional, moneybags! Can't cook? *Order Takeout, Asshole!*

Now, OTA should be utilized with care. It is *not* an excuse to constantly shirk your duties, particularly if you're actually ordering takeout and draining your household food budget to do so. It's a last-ditch option for when you really, really don't have the time or ability to make a decent meal, or whatever chore you're trying to avoid.

There are also tasks that you may both hate—like cleaning the house—that might be worth taking off of *both* of your plates permanently, if you have the budget. They might even be worth *making* the budget for. After a motorcycle accident severely limited the use of my right wrist for nine months, I became addicted to delivery laundry. I lived in NYC, so laundry was already something done in a laundromat or dropped off, but once necessity drove me to discover that Waverly Wu would actually come to my apartment, get the laundry, do it, and drop it off on a day of my choice no more than three business days after pickup... I'd found something for which I was willing to substitute two meals a week with Ramen noodles. I no longer need such services both because I have a husband who likes doing laundry and a washing machine in the apartment (and yes, I do about 10 percent of the laundry), but the point is that there are some chores that might just suck for you both and are worth considering if they can be permanently outsourced. If not, a fifty-fifty split is probably your best bet.

If even after all of this, your partner cries "cultural/familial differences" and refuses to take on their fair share of chores... it's time to have a serious sit down conversation, or even discuss it with a counselor. Trust me—it may seem like something small, but the accumulation of resentment over an uneven relationship is something that won't simply vanish.

So, in conclusion: **for the greatest feeling of equity, do what you like or are good at 80 percent of the time. Let your partner pick up the other 20 percent.**

Gremlins Are Real

I have a secret for you: Gremlins are real. And don't feed them after midnight.[44]

No, seriously, though—gremlins haunt our household. Have you ever put something down somewhere very specific only to have it disappear later? Have you ever definitely saved a delicious morsel to be eaten later only to be disappointed when you open the fridge that night? Or perhaps you absolutely wrote the time and date for a doctor's appointment on a pad of paper by the phone (going old-school here, I know) only to find the page has been torn off?

Your spouse swears up and down, front and back, sideways and crossways that they didn't move the thing, eat the snack, or tear off the page. Only you don't have any kids, haven't had any guests, and your pet doesn't have opposable thumbs.

This is a really, really easy way to fall into bickering or arguing, a classic example of each person *knowing* they are right when either one of you simply has to be wrong or our foundational understanding of physics has to shift.

I offer a third solution: Believe in gremlins.

The point is that so often these inconveniences are simply

only that—inconvenient. They don't actually harm anyone. Obviously, I'm not talking about something like moving your spouse's passport to a new drawer the night before they are getting up for a five a.m. flight or eating the last piece of treasured candy you can only get in your home country. Them's grounds for divorce! Kidding—sort of. But those two examples are things that a partner should actually consider before casually moving items or chowing down, because they're more important or meaningful things.

I'm talking about the time when I put my razor on the sink to make sure I packed it before our trip. I know with 100 percent certainty that I did this. Adam knows beyond a shadow of a doubt that he didn't move it. And yet, *somehow*, the razor was found tucked away in a toiletry basket.

Obviously, one of us mis-remembered either getting it out or moving it—and it's such a relatively unimportant thing that it's totally conceivable that either one of us did something on autopilot without noticing at all. But instead of arguing about it, we decided on a different course of action: to blame the household gremlin and move on.

I put the razor on the sink. Adam didn't touch it. The gremlin snuck in and moved it, but together we defeated him and found it and we both got to shave the things that needed shaving on our trip.

The point is that this mystery just wasn't something important enough to dwell on, but without the gremlin excuse, it's definitely not impossible that it could have escalated into an argument that had nothing to do with the razor, something about mutual distrust or the need to be believed no matter what or any number of unreasonable spirals.

The human brain really likes explanations. It does not like challenges to its understanding of reality and it does like to be believed.

I remember putting the razor on the sink. That is a real memory that I have to this day, even if it didn't happen—and I think we've all watched enough *Law & Order* to know that the mind can actually create memories. Despite that, *I also want my partner to believe me* when I say I put the razor on the sink.

But the fact is that the razor was not on the sink, so either I remember incorrectly or I'm accusing Adam of lying about not moving it or worse, challenging his ability to remember something accurately, which taps into his very real vein of fear around aging and cognitive ability.

An aside on that: Often, the fights at the end of a spiral are legitimate concerns or problems that can and should be worked out. I think we've all had the experience of thinking we're fighting about one thing only to end up six counties, a state line, and the Mississippi over, wondering how we got there. I'm certainly not saying that Adam and I shouldn't talk about his fears and vulnerabilities around memory, just that those are conversations that can be had in a saner, calmer environment and context than when we're packing up our things for a vacation.

Because oftentimes the gremlin strikes when we're already in compromised or vulnerable states: we're tired, we're hungry, we're stressed, we're rushed. Those aren't the times to dive into foundational questions of trust or understanding.

Blame the gremlin, have a snack, and see if it's worth bringing up whatever little sensitive spot got poked later... but for the time being, just throw your hands up, complain together about the nasty little gremlin, and move on.

As it turns out, the fact is that **not every mystery needs a logical solution**. Sometimes, you can just agree to have differing memories or experiences and it doesn't have to blow up into a huge debate about trust or the reliability of your partner's memory. Sometimes, it's just not that big a deal—so find a funny or silly way to defuse a potential situation before it can heat up.

And anyway, I like to imagine a cute little mogwai zipping around the apartment and teasing our cat.

PROPOSED LA COPPIA UTOPIA MASCOT

Say Thank You Every Day

When I was about twelve, my school brought a Holocaust survivor into our classroom to give a talk. At the time, I lived in Germany, so had heard a lot more about the Holocaust at this point in my life than your average non-Jewish American twelve-year-old, but I really wasn't prepared for the emotional impact of this man's story. I don't remember any of the details, but I do remember his main theme: gratitude.

Years of oppression in Germany, time spent in concentration camps, the loss of his family and much of his dignity, and the man's ultimate takeaway wasn't rage or frustration or vengeance, which would have all been entirely justified.

It was *gratitude*.

I think about gratitude a lot in the context of relationships.

I'm shocked by how often I notice a lack of gratitude—or at least, *expressed* gratitude—from individuals in a relationship. Familiarity not only breeds contempt, it also breeds forgetfulness: When someone cares for you consistently, it becomes woven into the pattern of your lives. This can be beautiful, but it can also render that care invisible against the louder concerns of everyday life. It can lead to complacency, and we can begin to take our partners for granted.

A *thank you* costs nothing, never hurts, and pretty much always helps. And when you're in situations of extra tension—such as those many expats face regularly—it can be a simple and free way to show your love and support for your partner.

Adam and I actively thank each other every day. I won't lie; it felt a little silly at first. But there's nothing like the look of giddy surprise on your partner's face when they realize that you've noticed something you'd usually take for granted.

If you're in a challenging moment with your spouse where you feel you are the one who is constantly unappreciated or unacknowledged, it can be hard to take the step to be the one to begin expressing thanks regularly. A common refrain I hear from (mostly female) friends is how frustrating it is to be expected to take care of certain things—managing housework, caring for children, balancing it all with their jobs—as a matter of course, only for their male partners to be actively applauded for doing the exact same things.[45] Or worse, when partners expect a pat on the head for doing something that should be a given, like helping to keep the home clean or picking up dinner or wiping off the bathroom sink. If there is a serious imbalance in your relationship in this way, it really deserves to be addressed through deep and honest conversation, or even with a counselor if needed.

But if you're simply noticing a lack of appreciation and expression of care, the fact is that you can only control your own actions, and gratitude is something that has a multiplying effect when utilized.

A thank you isn't just a pat on the head—it's also an extended hand. Just as an "I love you" can inspire an "I love you, too," a "thank you" can spark the partner's consideration of their own relationship with gratitude, and the things in their life for which they are grateful.

Make gratitude a habit and your relationship will reap the rewards a thousandfold.

Say thank you.

Even for something small, like filling up your partner's water bottle.

Even for something basic, like cleaning up after oneself.

Even for something expected, like a chore you're supposed to do anyway.

For expats, there can be so much going on—so much new stimulus to take in, so many strange customs to adapt to, so much culture shock—that gratitude is a really easy element to let fall by the wayside.

If verbal *thank yous* aren't your thing—and look, different love languages are real—there are all kinds of ways to show your partner that you care about them. You can leave them a note. You can give them more hugs. You can do an extra chore. You can play fun little games—about six months ago, I started texting Adam the same amount of emojis as the number in the current time; for example, at 5:55 he'll get five hearts or octopi. I don't sit around waiting for the time to show up, it's just a nice little way to remind him that I think of him when it happens.

I have truly come to believe that it is gratitude that is the soil from which every other good feeling grows, including love.

Acknowledge the Days of Defeat

There are days when, despite the lure of the sunny piazzas and the creamy cappuccinos and the soul-lifting facades, I don't leave our apartment and refuse to pick up my phone for any unknown number.

Obviously, this is something of a luxury because I work from home, but I think everyone—living abroad or not—can relate to this feeling: of having had *enough* and wanting to burrow deep into blankets and books and cats and pretend absolute invulnerability to the influences of the outside world.

I call these Days of Defeat, and they are surprisingly hard to talk about.

Why, you might ask? While it might seem like such a universal experience could easily be shared and discussed, it's not that simple.

When you move abroad, your friends split into two categories: the ones who live in your new home and the ones who don't.

For the ones who don't, whom you've perhaps left behind in

your home country, it can be absolutely inconceivable to spend a single day not basking in the glory of your adopted country. Remember those cappuccinos I mentioned? They actually really are that good, so if your distant friends have never themselves lived—not traveled, *lived*—in a foreign country, they may not exactly be open to hearing about how hard it is for you, what with the abundance of cheap, high quality wine, easy access to magnificent works of art, or the ability to hop on a train and be in Paris in six hours for twenty bucks. So when you need to vent, they're out.

For the friends who are living near you, these can be further divided into two categories: people who are also expats or immigrants and people who are from the place where you are currently living. The former might be your best bet for expressing your difficult moments, though be careful not to turn it into a habit. Misery usually just begets more misery, and there's a difference between a healthy vent and destructive spiraling.

Unfortunately, friends who are from your new country can also be a challenging audience for your woes: after all, your adoptive country is their home country, and blows feel harder when aimed closer to the chest. Or in the immortal words of Viserys Targaryen from *House of the Dragon*, "I will speak of my brother as I wish. You will not."

Many immigrants and expats are met with a cold, "if you don't like it, you can go back home" when they express anger or frustration, which is both alienating and unhelpful (especially if you are an immigrant who is unable to return to your home country).

Without being able to talk about it, without the support of

friends... it's pretty easy to start to feel guilty when you're un-happy in a new place. It becomes a pretty slippery slope down to a pretty self-deprecating and miserable place.

So I'm here to confirm the following for you:

It is perfectly 100 percent natural and expected to experience frustration and anger with parts of your new home, and it doesn't make you an ungrateful or ignorant person to feel those feelings.

Is it healthy to feel them all of the time? No, and you might need to seek out regular outlets for your feelings like therapy or a support group if you're constantly miserable most of the time. But if you're just simply feeling particularly grumpy one day? I've gotcha covered: Take a Day of Defeat.

Take that day "off" of your adoptive country to the extent that you possibly can. Stay in your home, or go to a park alone.

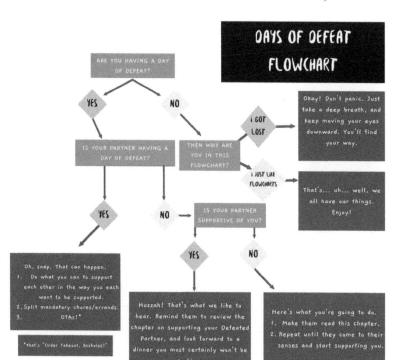

What does this have to do with relationships? Well, if you're lucky enough to be on your expat journey with a partner, it means that they can help you—or you can help them—with a Day of Defeat. No matter which partner you are, here are a few ground rules:

1. The Defeated Partner is not expected to engage in their non-native language, even if it's the language you usually use at home (this is especially important for couples where one is from the adoptive country).

1. This means no errands. No asking them to run to the grocery store or enoteca. It doesn't matter how small it seems, sometimes engaging with the super nice checkout person who thinks it's delightful that a foreigner lives in her neighborhood is just too much. OTA.
2. The Defeated Partner also gets a pass on answering the doorbell for the day. It may sound like a small thing, but it can be the straw that broke the camel's back when you're already overloaded. I can't tell you how often I've had days when I've straight up ignored the doorbell because I just couldn't deal with even the idea of interacting with a presumably perfectly friendly delivery person.
3. If you're the supporting spouse, understand that the Defeated Partner may not want to answer their phone. If the Defeated Partner is expecting an important call, offer to answer their phone for them if it's something you can handle.
1. The Defeated Partner is exempt from any shaming or guilting: no snide questions about their canceled language lesson, no insistence that 'only practice will help' (*we know!*), no wondering aloud when that piece of bureaucratic nonsense will finally be dealt with.
2. Encourage the Defeated Partner to watch or read something comforting for them—maybe something from their home country, or play their favorite album.
3. The Defeated Partner is to receive lots of hugs (if that's their thing) and general support.

And if you're both having a Day of Defeat... divide, conquer, and try to laugh and support each other. To quote Scarlett O'Hara– "After all, tomorrow is another day."

Beware the Over Lean

"Lean On Me" isn't just a Bill Withers classic, it's also excellent marriage advice.

Generally speaking.

Unfortunately, there is such a thing as leaning too hard–what I call the dreaded Over Lean.

This is most common in couples where one person is foreign and one is native: The native partner finds themselves doing the lioness's share of certain tasks because they speak the language or the weight of socializing falls upon them because they have the connections or cultural awareness to navigate that arena with greater ease.

But it can also happen, as it has in my own marriage, when one partner is simply more effective in certain areas. Adam has a lot of skills, and while I won't say that he *can't* manage a schedule or paperwork—he runs his own business, after all—the fact of the matter is that watching him handle administrative issues feels, to me, like watching a puppy leap for a snack just out of reach. Adorable, but also a little frustrating and sad and definitely not the most efficient way to do things.

And honestly, it makes loads of sense to divide and conquer. We should lean into our strengths, right?

Yes... and no.

Just because something is faster or more efficient doesn't make it better.[46]

When one person is expected to handle one aspect of a couple's life all of the time, that relationship begins flirting with resentment and shame.

The resentment, of course, comes when one partner is doing 100 percent of anything.[47]

The shame, of course, comes when the other partner realizes this but feels helpless to do anything about it.

This situation can even come into play with couples who are, in theory, equally new to the new country.

Adam and I both started learning Italian at the exact same time—namely, the month we moved to Italy. But for whatever reason, the language came a little faster and more smoothly to me, though I'm still conversational at best. Mix that with the fact, as stated earlier, that I'm typically the organizer and planner in our relationship, and we quickly found ourselves in an Over Lean situation that built as a slow simmer I was unaware of until it boiled over.

The boiling point occurred when I came down with covid and we had to go to the emergency room somewhere around day ten of really intense symptoms. The nurse checking us in asked us several questions in rapid-fire Italian, and instead of trying to answer the questions or asking her to slow down, my (not sick) husband looked at me.

Me, who had barely been able to make the half-mile walk

to the hospital. Me, who had been fighting fevers and swollen lymph nodes and headaches and the worst sore throat of my life for almost two weeks at that point. Me, who was sicker than I can ever remember being since I was stuck in the rainforest in Peru a two hours' boat journey from the nearest doctor with nothing but two buckets, a bottle of Inca Cola, and a very, very kind and concerned friend to hold my hair.

Under normal circumstances, I actually take pride in my competency and independence. I *like* when others trust me to get things done. I was complicit in creating this circumstance, where Adam looked to me for support in confusing or overwhelming situations.

But I really, really did *not* want to be responsible for communicating about my illness in Italian, not with a perfectly good and generally quite capable husband standing next to me. I remember a strange sensation of simultaneously sinking into despair and raising my hackles in anger as Adam's desperate eyes searched mine for the answers to the nurse's questions.[48]

That experience was a bit of the straw that broke the camel's back. Fortunately, it led to a really fruitful discussion about both that specific moment as well as a broader look at our distribution of responsibilities and expectations.

Unsurprisingly, as it turns out, Adam dislikes being overly dependent on my shitty Italian as much as I do. He resolved to work harder on his Italian and we agreed to put more money into lessons for him—a great example, I think, of how not *everything* in a relationship has to be exactly equal. Adam needs lessons with a real human teacher; I can learn by reading Harry Potter in Italian.

Here are two concrete steps you can take to combat the Over Lean:

1. Encourage the Leaner to actively develop their skills in the area of concern and make that a priority for the relationship. As described, in our case, Adam really stepped up on his language learning by pursuing and scheduling iTalki lessons and increasing Duolingo usage.

2. Delegate tasks for the Leaner to deal with completely independently. In our situation, Adam handles online ordering and as a result deals with conversations on the phone with companies or in person with mail carriers. We've also agreed on specific tasks for him to own, such as getting our shutters fixed. That meant finding a company that could do it, contacting them, sorting out payment, arranging for measurements to be taken and the final installation scheduled—all in Italian. I didn't even look at the paint chips.

The second point is particularly important and a huge relief for the Leaned Upon partner, but of course it comes with one major caveat: if you have mutually decided on tasks or responsibilities to be entirely owned by one person in the partnership, the other person has to accept *how* their partner wants to achieve the goal. No micromanaging. No complaining. No implying that *you* could have done it better. That's kind of the point.

Believe me, I know it's hard not to express it when you believe you could do something more effectively; I'm the insufferable queen of the raised eyebrow and thoughtful sigh.

But unless you're looking at an error that will cost significant money, hours, or sanity... *just let them do it.*[49] People learn through experience.

Remember: The goal here isn't *just* to accomplish a particular task. It's also to help a Leaner gain confidence and learn to navigate their new environment. Ultimately, that is what will best serve the relationship.

Find Friends

Don't get me wrong: it's hard to make friends as an adult under the best of circumstances: we're all busy, we're all tired, we've all found much easier coping mechanisms to unwind, like a book or a PS5. Sure, it might be cool to meet someone new, but what if you get five hangouts into the friendship only to realize they're a Nintendo person? Yeah, you get it.

But doing so with a language and cultural barrier is even harder, exponentially so.

Forging friendships is an area of immense sensitivity, angst, and sadness for many individuals who live abroad. It's also one of those areas that can be easily dismissed or overlooked, because I think our society generally undervalues and underappreciates the importance of friendships in their own right, but also their role in supporting a healthy relationship.

Humans evolved to live in packs. We thrive in community. And while it's a magical and special thing to have a partner who has chosen you as their Number One Person, human beings need more than that. We need variety in our socialization, and it's human nature to crave fresh opinions. Like, I know that Adam *of course* thinks I'm one of the funniest people he knows, but I kinda take that for granted sometimes. His laugh is the sweetest to elicit, but sometimes I just want the satisfaction of an unexpected guffaw from a near-stranger.

By developing healthy friendships outside of the context of your relationship, you'll actually be bolstering the relationship itself, both by keeping a healthy flow of external influences (how can you find new opinions to share or stories to tell if you never interact with other people?) and by preventing codependence from creeping into your relationship.

Codependence—the uglier cousin of the Over Lean—is a very real problem for a lot of people, but especially in the expat world.

Below I've outlined a few common problems specific to expats with regards to making friends in their new home.

Seeing Through The Mystique

If you have friends who have never traveled and who are dissatisfied with their home country or state, for whatever reason, there can sometimes be something of a mystique around foreign countries, particularly Europe—there's a sense that things are *better* there, that people are generally cooler.[50]

I've seen first hand the shock when my American peers studying abroad at Oxford were faced with the harsh reality that UK universities are just as much Slytherin as Gryffindor.

The unfortunate fact of our world is that there are idiots and assholes everywhere.

Your bigoted cousin? A version of him exists in your new country.

Your interfering neighbor? A version of her exists in your new country.

Your mom's nosy church friend? A version of them exists in your new country.

Your fellow yogi who keeps trying to get you to sign up for this week's MLM? A version of her exists in your new country.

All of the people you hate have counterparts in your new country.

Proceed with caution.

The Unscalable Wall

You know how so many people you know stayed in their hometown and still hang out with the same people they always did and go to the same bars that let them sneak a drink at sixteen?

Yeah, those people also exist wherever you've moved, and it's *tough* to break into that fortress.

I also know those people. In a way, Adam *was* that person. When we met on a dating app in 2019, I quickly dazzled him with my knowledge of a version of Nashville, his hometown, that he had no idea existed, because when he'd moved back in 2017, he'd slid right back into his old patterns.

You see, I was in many ways an expat to Nashville, a curious outsider from New York City who, despite an American passport, hadn't grown up in the States and had no clue what the deal was outside of the two coasts. So I saw the city with fresh eyes, lived in a super trendy[51] neighborhood that younger Adam had been warned about, and introduced him to the crop of newcomers moving into the city whom natives—or "unicorns," as they are called—are kinda salty about, but that's for another essay.

The point is that even if you're a well-traveled human of infinite curiosity, like Adam certainly is, it's really, really easy to fall into patterns forged in your youth.

This means that what many expats find, when they come to a new city or country, is that it's *really fucking hard* to make new friends among the local populace, because you've got the double whammy of the inherent difficulty of making new friends as a busy adult combined with the language/cultural barrier.

It doesn't mean people don't want to be your friend. It's not anything personal, usually.

It just means that it's hard to scale that particular wall and get into the inner sanctum. It takes diligence and a lot of hard work.

The Judgement of Exprats

You know what doesn't help when you're trying to make friends? When people make you feel bad about where you're hunting for them.

I'm sure most of us have encountered this type: the holier-than-thou veteran expats (shall we call them... *exprats*?) who give you shit for being friends with other expats.

Common refrains of the exprat:

"I hardly know any other expats."

"I can't stand the expat community."

"Why bother living abroad if you're just going to spend time with other foreigners?"

They generally say all of this with the sanctimonious and judgemental—yet somehow also *co-conspiratorial*[52]—tones of a chronic dieter who assumes that of course *you* understand the evils of carbohydrates. Like, *no*, you can pry my croissant out of my cold, dead hands, Barbara. "We" are not in agreement on this.

Look: I understand the sentiment to a certain degree. Sometimes, the expat community consists of embarrassingly drunk twenty-somethings, and I need my friends to be able to ~~hold their liquor~~ not be an embarrassment to our home country. And it's true that sometimes, people lose out on a fuller, richer experience of their adoptive country because of their nervousness or fear when it comes to making local friends.

But having expat friends doesn't preclude having local friends. And beyond that, having only expat friends for a while as you get your bearings doesn't mean that's how it's always going to be in the future!

When you first get somewhere and are just settling in, it's kind of like triage. You want to feel settled and comfortable STAT, and one of the best ways to do that is to make some friends. If you don't speak the local language, well... you need to fish in the pond for which you have the right equipment. Don't worry, you can always branch out when you get some new poles.

But even beyond that, I do take issue with the snobbery of avoiding expat friends.

I'll let you in on one of my dirty little secrets: *I actually like other expats.*

I grew up a Third Culture Kid, outside of the culture of either of my parents. It's a unique experience, as is living in a foreign country as an adult.

You know what a lot of locals you meet living abroad haven't done? *Lived abroad in a foreign country.*

Typically, when we look for friends, we look for individuals with whom we can share a common bond: a shared history, experience, or interest. This is why so many people you know from home still hang out with the same dweebs from high school. Hell, even Harry and Ron didn't warm up to Hermione until they had to deal with that whole bathroom troll situation. You may not have a bathroom troll, but you do have an "uproot your life and plop yourself in new soil" situation going on. Kinda similar, when you think about it.

You're very likely to have a lot in common with other expats —not just a language, but an outlook on life or an adventurous spirit or even just some much-needed sympathy because they've been in your friendless shoes before, too. When you're desperate, a friendship born out of pity is better than no friendship at all.[53]

So don't let anyone make you feel bad about making friends wherever you're able (or wherever you prefer). Making friends is hard enough without adding unnecessary barriers.

But *how*, I hear you ask? *How do I make these friends? Do I just drag the likeliest looking human to the nearest coffee shop and force them to drink a cappuccino with me as we laugh uproariously over some inane joke? Do I adopt a dog from the shelter after ensuring it passes the strictest standards of Cuteness and Friendliness, hoping it will lure in strangers who have no idea that I'm harboring a deep well of loneliness??*

As I began writing a section about this, I realized that, frankly, this is a topic for a whole 'nother book—the next one in the Expat Guidebook series: The Expat Friendship Guidebook.

Family

Family family family.

We all have plenty to say about our families, but whatever we say is rarely untainted by an added "but..."

As in, "I love them so much, but..." or "I can't stand them, but..."

Basically, **families are complicated no matter what, and for expats it becomes exponentially more complicated.** Love 'em or not, families who are far away are both easier and harder to deal with. And the ones that "just don't get your lifestyle choices" are a pretty significant source of consistent additional stress.[54]

Managing the family you left back home could (and will!) be an entire book in and of itself: Believe me, we know. There are bound to be some hurt feelings if you put an ocean or a continent between yourself and your family no matter your reason for doing so (for love, for a job, just because you felt like it).

At the end of the day, though, no matter why you are where you are, it's important to remember two things:

1. Your choices are your own, and only you are responsible for them.

2. You can't control how your family feels about said choices.

So whether your family is unsupportive because they hate or fear foreign countries or simply because they were basically always going to disapprove of anything you do,[55] there are some basic guidelines you can follow to mitigate the situation, and hopefully even lay the groundwork for a healthy relationship.

Align On Your Approach and Set Expectations

It goes without saying that as a couple, your approach to parents and in-laws should be aligned and you should always and without fail have each other's backs.

I highly recommend an approach where each partner takes point on handling their own parents: There's a lot of knowledge and history there that can help with understanding motivations and potential reactions, and it tends to be easier for parents to forgive their child than that child's spouse should a sensitive subject be broached.

Ultimately, the point here is that you are two people standing side by side tackling problems *together*. Strategize and align, and for goodness' sake, *listen to your partner* if they tell you there's a problem with the in-laws!

When you've aligned your approach to dealing with family, it's of paramount importance to set clear expectations and boundaries with them.

1. Educate them on how best to communicate with you.
    1. Do they know about Whatsapp? Can you help them

download it? We gifted Adam's elderly uncle an iPhone before we left and made sure it was Face-Time ready. We spend a not-insignificant amount of time seeing his ear, but he loves it!

2. If you are anxious about video calls, let them know how often you can handle that: once a week? A month? Only at holidays? Would you talk to them more if it's just a voice chat?

3. Are you open to your family following your social media? Instagram, Snapchat, or Facebook posts (showing my age here, I know) or even a full-blown blog (*really* showing my age here!) can be a great way for people to feel more incorporated into your day-to-day life.

2. Share what they can expect from you in terms of communication.

1. Make sure they know what the time zone differences are (and if or how Daylight Savings affects them), and what your work schedule is.

2. Are you more of a texter or a caller? It doesn't hurt to be explicit.

3. Be clear about your plans for visiting. Give them something to look forward to—or avoid getting their hopes up.

Never JADE

JADE is a delightful acronym I came across in the wilds of the internet and have incorporated into almost all of my advice to friends dealing with frustrating families. It stands for Justify, Argue, Defend, or Explain.

When you embark upon life as an adult, you become responsible for yourself and lose the need to justify, argue, defend, or explain your choices to just about anyone until such time as you choose to invite someone into that circle—and that invitation can look like a marriage proposal, a business partnership, or taking on debts.

The point is that, at the end of the day, your in-laws and parents are not really entitled to JADE. Frankly, if and when you engage in JADE actions, it often only implies you're willing to discussing things further.

By offering justification, you imply your decision needs to be justified.

By presenting an argument, you give permission to provide a counter-argument.

By defending, you're vulnerable to attack.

By explaining, you imply the conversation is open.

Now, there are circumstances in which you can *choose* to explain yourself, and that can be a very healthy choice.

Once, in the context of a family counseling session, we opened up the arena to discuss our impending move. I was honestly surprised by the result: Beyond the expected frustrations and anxieties about our decision to move overseas, my in-laws were also feeling an element of fear surrounding one area I hadn't considered at all: our financial security.

You see, their presumption was that we were basically just taking a long vacation. This was actually a pretty reasonable presumption for their culture: Where they're from, people rarely just up and move overseas. Going abroad is for holidays, not for *living*. As a person who grew up moving frequently, it hadn't ever occurred to me that this might be an area of concern. *Of course* we were going to be working!

As such, it was actually a very reasonable fear of theirs that Adam would stall his career or we'd spend all of our savings by traveling. Because we were able to uncover this nugget of insight, Adam and I were able to explain to them that we were actually going to be working while we traveled, and would not be halting our careers. In fact, we ended up moving to a place with a lower cost of living. We're saving more now than ever before!

The important part of this, though, is that we *chose* to explain. They were not entitled to it, and it was something given freely in the context of a calm conversation because we care about them and wanted to achieve some harmony—it wasn't an exasperated volley after a fight or endless needling.

It can be hard to maintain these boundaries, but they are critical to building and maintaining a healthy relationship. When the family understands that you're not going to JADE, the whole dynamic changes.

Stick To A Reasonable Amount of Venting

I love venting. When I was a kid and my mom used to ask me how my day at school was, I'd give her the whooooooole download. Once, she asked me how I could be so *negative*, and I was stunned. You see, I didn't think I was being negative at all. It wasn't *my* fault that the kids I went to school with were troglodytes. I was just reporting the facts, neutral as the AP.

The point is that as much as I loathe toxic positivity, overwhelming negativity can really get you down, too. Even if both of you agree that your partner's parents are frustrating, there are a couple of good reasons to limit your venting:

1. It can ignite shame and/or defensiveness in your partner: This is their family, where they come from. There is not a person on the planet with a functioning relationship with their family who likes to have their nose rubbed in its flaws by an outsider. And though the new family unit you two have created should take precedence over the family of origin, that family is still important and it's natural for your partner to feel defensive of it.

2. If your partner is constantly feeling like they need to defend their family of origin, they have little room to complain themselves. Ideally, you should create a safe space for one another to express how you each feel, and if your partner believes expressing their frustrations might simply lead to you piling on all the time... well, they might refrain from doing it at all, and then you're in a situation where you can't be honest with each other. This is not good.

It's a wonderful thing to be able to be open and honest with your partner, but as ever, it's important to be mindful of what you're putting into your relationship on the daily.

Be Empathetic and Find Ways to Bridge the Gap

Technology really is a beautiful thing—I (just barely) remember the days of phone cards and predetermined call times. Now, we have cell phones that can call a different country anytime without racking up hundreds of dollars in fees, *and* we can even call with *live video!* The future is now, and thank goodness, because it allows us to accommodate the varying needs of our families.

Still, despite this great equalizer—my and Adam's respective parents have different communication styles.

My father is a little more integrated into my daily life—we casually chat on the phone a few times a week, usually for ten or twenty minutes, occasionally longer. His wife, my stepmother Pam, and Adam are sometimes around when we talk and they'll chime in occasionally, but it's largely one-to-one communication, which I prefer.

Adam's parents, on the other hand, like to do a full blown video conference sit down for about an hour every week.

At first, I was a bit resistant to this. I don't really like video calls in the first place, and I really don't like sitting down for long conversations with big groups, which I always find a little awkward. I mean, I have to go through enough Zoom meetings for work! One on one is a different story, of course, but I still don't prefer video calls.

But I reached into my well of empathy and realized how important this time is for them. I think for them, it is simply more meaningful to make our calls feel more like dedicated time actively spent together (as compared to my calls with my dad, which are often conducted while I'm walking or doing something else and frequently get cut off because one of us has to go). I think of it now as if it were a lunch date, like we'd have if we lived closer. This realization made me much happier to indulge their preferences, because I can understand the joy it brings them.

Now, daily communication styles are one thing, but the real sticking point for expat family relationships comes with *visits*.

Who does the visiting, and how frequently? Who pays for the visits?

This is a really important question to settle within your own relationship before you make your intentions and boundaries clear to your families.

You see, our situation right now is not really fair.

My in-laws find travel challenging—which is reasonable—and don't have a natural interest in it. They haven't yet come to visit us, but within our first two years of living in Italy, my father and Pam will have visited us twice for over two weeks each time. We've also been back to the US for two family visits since we moved. But this means that my family has gotten *twice as many visits*, twice as much real, in-person time. I know my in-laws would love more time with us. It isn't really fair, but these are choices made on both sides.

And beyond that—for Adam and I, our priority simply isn't to use any and all travel time and funds for family visits. I've been back to the States one additional time solo to officiate a friend's wedding and saw no family during that quick weekend. Adam and I are also going on a month-long trip to Vietnam and Thailand over one winter holiday because I've always wanted to go and the timing is right.

I can empathize with and understand why some family might be hurt that we've made these choices. It's not an unreasonable feeling to be upset that we're spending time and money to go somewhere new instead of to see family.

But while it's not an unreasonable feeling, it *is* an unreasonable expectation.

When Adam and I moved abroad, we knew that part of the cost would be seeing family less. It's not that it was an easy price to pay: We don't *not* want to see our families, but discovery, curiosity, and exploration expressed through travel are values that mean a lot to us both as individuals and as a couple. So we knew that not only would we be moving abroad, but we also wouldn't be going back to the States more than once per year, barring emergencies.

But the fact is that our values make us who we are, and we're better people—better spouses, better friends, a better son and daughter—as a result of living in alignment with these values, whether others can see that or not.

Together, we had to determine what our boundaries were and discuss how to make our families feel loved and included to the best of our abilities despite those boundaries. We try to make our families feel heard and cared for—phone calls, care packages (or postcards and stickers if larger packages are too expensive!), an hour a week for video calls are all choices we make to show we care.

It's not enough. Of *course* it's not enough. The saddest fact of being human is that there is never enough time with the people we love. But it's what we can do within the context of the life we need to live to be our happiest, best selves, and that's all anyone can do at the end of the day.

One of the universal truths that binds humans together no matter what culture we come from is that navigating one's family can be like walking a tightrope. This doesn't have anything to do with how much we love them, of course—it's simply a result of putting multiple humans in emotional proximity. And when you add in families of different cultures? Get ready for the Netflix holiday special.

The most important thing for expat couples to remember with regards to dealing with family issues—hell, the most important thing for expat couples to remember, full stop—is this: When you commit to someone, you are signing up to be on their team. Work together, consult with each other, and you'll find strength in navigating these waters... *together*.

Conclusion

I hope you've found *The Expat Marriage Guidebook* helpful—and more than that, I hope you had as much fun reading it as I had writing it. Perhaps the most surprising revelation for me while writing this book was just how much overlap there is between the advice I'd give to expat couples and the advice I'd give to my married friends who live in their hometowns.

At its most basic, fundamental level, a healthy relationship is defined by the satisfaction and well-being of the individuals within the relationship itself, full stop. While expats can and do face unique problems and stresses, the truth is that all relationships face conflict and tension. Whether you need to take a Day of Defeat due to cultural overwhelm or just plain life overwhelm, effective and open communication coupled with kindness and a generous spirit are truly the number one keys to a strong partnership.[56]

But in the wild world of living abroad, there are so many nuances and quirks and unexpected turns that arise that having a strong partnership can become uniquely important in your life. Having a solid co-navigator in rough seas is never a bad thing.

As a cheat sheet, I've taken what I think are the most

important takeaways from each of the chapters and collected them for you below:

Being pragmatic is the most romantic thing you can do for your partner because it is adequately preparing for your road ahead.

It's absolutely critical to get on the same page about the bread as soon as humanly possible if you're considering being lifelong sandwich buddies.

Ultimately, when unconditional love is the gauge for relationship health and viability, we trap ourselves into feeling that a failure to love *no matter what*, even if we're miserable, is a reflection of our own failure as a spouse.

Your daily life does not consist of your wedding day over and over and over.

The trick is knowing when to stay and do the work to try to fix something you care about and when to cut your losses and skedaddle with whatever you haven't sunk into the relationship—even if it means leaving behind the precious things you've already given up.

At the end of the day, it doesn't really matter what cultural norms are: What matters is how you and your partner each feel within the context of the specific relationship that you are tending.

We all suck in some way or another.

Resentment is not a guest you want to entertain.

We can't change what others feel—and in point of fact, we also can't change what *we* feel. But what we can change is our relationship to our own feelings, how we react, and what we do.

Couples who work mindfully through their problems with

the help of a professional can come through them—even infidelity, even cultural clashes—much stronger for it.

Remember the stranger you fell in love with every single day.

The Expat Tax is incurred even when you don't necessarily do anything *wrong*... and all you can do is make your peace with this fact of expat life.

For the greatest feeling of equity, do what you like or are good at [in terms of household chores] 80 percent of the time. Let your partner pick up the other 20 percent.

Not every mystery needs a logical solution. Sometimes, you can just blame the gremlin and move on.

Make gratitude a habit and your relationship will reap the rewards a thousandfold.

It is perfectly 100 percent natural and expected to experience frustration and anger with parts of your adopted culture, and it doesn't make you an ungrateful or ignorant person to feel those feelings.

Unless you're looking at an error that will cost significant money, hours, or sanity... let a dependent Leaner take charge of some things and do them in their own way!

By developing healthy friendships outside of the context of your relationship, you'll actually be bolstering the relationship itself.

Families are complicated no matter what, and for expats it becomes exponentially more complicated.

If you enjoyed this book, I'd love to hear from you—what you thought about the book, topics you'd like to hear more about, or your own stories of being in a relationship abroad. Sign up for the newsletter at lacoppiautopia.com, or you can join in the conversation at the facebook group, Utopians Unite! And don't forget to leave a review. Thanks for joining me on this journey!

Acknowledgements

Writing *The Expat Marriage Guidebook* has been an absolutely joyous whirlwind, one that wouldn't have happened without the help of several individuals.

Madeleine Calvi's editorial assessment of the earliest draft of this book greatly influenced and strengthened the structure and direction of the whole shebang. Also, you have them to thank (or blame) for inspiring me to create most of the illustrations.

Emily Heddleson went way, way above and beyond as a proofreader and a friend. I truly value her insight, skills, and friendship!

My sister, Cristina Romagnoli, has been my number one cheerleader and shadow self for as long as I can remember. I wouldn't be me without her and this world would be like a billion times worse without her in it.

If I got my tricks from anyone, it was definitely Julian Romagnoli. The easiest way to have healthy relationships? Be raised by this guy and *pay attention* to what he says—or doesn't say, as the case can often be.

Kat Hargrave has not only been one of my dearest friends for over a decade, but also provided invaluable feedback and advice on the cover design.

Adriann Ranta is a stellar human who has always been incredibly generous with her knowledge and expertise about book stuff, even when I have dumb questions.

And, of course, my eternal love and appreciation for Adam Lofbomm, without whom this book literally wouldn't exist. I mean, it's a marriage book and we're married so... duh. In particular, I simply couldn't do without his support for every harebrained side project I cook up. And there are a *lot* of them. If you'd like to see more of our adventures in marriage, you can follow our instagram @la.coppia.utopia !

Appendix: Resources

Ashlinn's Recommendations
Books for self-growth

- *Meditations* by Marcus Aurelius
- *The Heroine's Journey* by Maureen Murdock
- *Meeting the Shadow* by Connie Zweig
- *The Body Keeps The Score* by Bessel van der Kolk
  Books about relationships
- *The New Rules of Marriage* by Terrance Real
- *All About Love* by bell hooks
- *Mating in Captivity* by Esther Perel
  Books about existing now
- *For Small Creatures Such As We* by Sasha Sagan
- *Tiny Beautiful Things* by Cheryl Strayed
- *It All Turns On Affection* by Wendell Berry
- *Tribe: On Homecoming and Belonging* by Sebastian Junger
- *Learning to Die in the Anthropocene* by Roy Scranton
- *All We Can Save* by Ayana Elizabeth Johnson and Katharine K. Wilkinson

Podcasts (some are also newsletters!)

- *Terrible, Thanks for Asking* by Nora McInerny
- *Where Shall We Begin?* by Esther Perel
- *Dear Sugars* by Cheryl Strayed
- *Living Myth* by Michael Meade
- *Savage Lovecast* by Dan Savage

Movies for Expats

- The Before Trilogy: *Before Sunrise, Before Sunset, Before Midnight*

Adam's Recommendations

Books for self-growth

- *A Joseph Campbell Companion: Reflections on the Art of Living* by Joseph Campbell
- *Grow Up: A Man's Guide to Masculine Emotional Intelligence* by Owen Marcus
- *You Were Born for This* by Chani Nicholas
- *The Gifts of Imperfection* by Brenè Brown
- *Transforming Fate Into Destiny* by Robert Ohotto
- *Iron John* by Robert Bly

Books about relationships

- *He, She, & We* (Trilogy) by Robert A. Johnson
- *The Art of Sexual Ecstasy* by Margo Anand

- *Codependent No More* by Melody Beattie
- *Getting the Love You Want* by Harville Hendrix
- *The Enneagram, Relationships and Intimacy: Understanding One Another Leads to Loving Better and Living More Fully* by David Daniels and Suzanne Dion

Books about existing now

- *Sapiens* by Yuval Noah Harari
- *The Wisdom of Insecurity* by Alan Watts
- *Vagabonding* by Rolf Potts
- *The 4 Hour Workweek* by Tim Ferris

Podcasts (some are also newsletters!)

- *The Daily Evolver* by Jeff Saltzman
- *Perennial Meditations* by J.W. Bertolotti
- *Derek Sivers Podcast*
- *The Marginalian* by Maria Popova

Footnotes

1. ^ You may recognize this in another word we use today: *travail*, which usually means "work, especially when arduous or involving painful effort" but, less commonly but far more disquietingly, actual child-birthing labor.

2. ^ Or any committed relationship. *Marriage* is just an easy way to shorthand the experiences of two people who have decided to throw in their lots together, so you'll see I use *partnership* and *marriage* interchangeably through this book.

3. ^ My dream, actually. I really want to learn to play the harmonica—it's my resolution for 2023, and I'm putting it here so all six people who read this book will hold me accountable in the coming months.

4. ^ This is not a joke.

5. ^ And I know you are out there, because I am one of you: I started reading Dan Savage and Esther Perel at age twelve.

6. ^ With apologies to the great Pat Benatar.

7. ^ I once went to a wedding where, no joke, a family friend of the bride called the groom a "nonentity." Which immediately became my favorite insult of all time.

8. ˆ Let's take a moment to learn from Adam's experiences as a man who was married not once but *twice* before we met. Both marriages were complete whirlwinds (as in, from meeting to marriage in a matter of months) driven by various external pressures and internal insecurities. But you can't run from your problems, nor can you marry them away. Our elopement in San Juan was sexy and romantic *because* of the immense amount of pragmatic work we did together and separately before saying "I do."

9. ˆ This can be okay, though—some of my favorite lunches were sandwich combos I wouldn't have necessarily put together on my own.

10. ˆ I feel pretty strongly about these not being sandwiches, but as a person of integrity I painfully acknowledge that people who do think this have a point. Even if they're wrong.

11. ˆ It surprises me how many people don't talk about kids before getting married, either out of thoughtlessness or because they come from a culture that simply assumes you'll at least *try*.

12. ˆ This can be a good option, because neither person has the "home field advantage," but it wouldn't work for all couples. Language is so important to me that I think I would find it challenging to be in a relationship where I couldn't speak English, though I speak other languages well enough. But everyone is different!

13. ˆ Expats in Germany, that one's for you!

14. ˆ I know: between this and the essay on how I refused to

promise to love Adam forever in our marriage vows, I'm not painting myself in the best light.

15. ˆ Two footnotes here: first, vegans should please feel free to substitute the non-animal cookie-enhancing product of their choice. Second, little baby Ashlinn was in fact once found eating sticks of butter. But you all know what I'm getting at here.

16. ˆ I once suggested to someone that an ideal life goal was to simply feel contentment. Her response was immediate and visceral . . . disgust, I think? The idea that we might strive simply to enjoy our lives instead of to constantly experience ecstatic bliss is another one I think we don't put enough stock in.

17. ˆ In fact, although I'm not a regular romance novel reader, I think the way society maligns romance novels is more about a general disregard for so-called "women-centric" literature than a disdain for the content itself.

18. ˆ If this is a spoiler for you, I'm not sorry. Even though 1997 *feels* like it was only a couple of years ago, I'm sorry to say it's actually been *more than twenty*, which is the universally accepted minimum for releasing one from spoiler concerns.

19. ˆ This is a true scenario based on my real grandparents.

20. ˆ Roughly 2006. Three years LDR, whoop whoop!

21. ˆ Italy is one of the only countries where you can have two phone numbers on one SIM card... no need for a burner phone for that affair!

22. ˆ I solemnly swear I have never done this. Please don't revoke my passport.

23. ˆ The answer to this, by the way, is NO. No, you cannot. Adam tried this once at a restaurant in our Italian city and the waitress literally refused to serve him.

24. ˆ I'm on good terms with all of my other exes. Just not this one.

25. ˆ And I have them in spades... I may not be emotive, but I am deeply emotional.

26. ˆ Or at least, it was. I do believe he's come to appreciate its unique flavor, but it was initially jarring.

27. ˆ If you're not American and don't know what Four Loko is, I'm going to leave you in ignorance here. It is one of the great shames of my people.

28. ˆ Or, if you can, please get in touch. I've got plans for you!

29. ˆ I read a book recently set in the middle ages where an elderly man hadn't seen his reflection in decades. Decades! Oh, the freedom...

30. ˆ Well, I guess we're all technically actively dying, but I like to make sure I'm not doing so faster than expected.

31. ˆ There's no award, this is my way of tricking people who think they couldn't benefit from therapy into going to therapy.

32. ˆ A Dan Savage-ism for Dump The MotherFucker Already.

33. ˆ In retrospect, thinking about it now, it's possible that a big part of our success so far is just how damn determined we are to make it work.

34. ˆ A tune he quickly changed when he realized that just because a partnership isn't a marriage doesn't mean it isn't serious!

35. ˆ No, seriously—I encourage you to learn more about Marilyn Monroe, who had a fascinating and tragic life.

36. ˆ Reasonable for them, not me, obviously.

37. ˆ In fact, I like to joke that Adam literally never shuts up: He talks for a living, talks with me all day, and also talks in his sleep.

38. ˆ Which, frankly, would have been entirely reasonable considering that you cannot buy bus tickets online nor anywhere but the tabaccheria, the opening hours of which are entirely dependent upon the whim of the cantankerous old man who has been selling cigarettes in that same shop for the last thousand years.

39. ˆ Also, I'm the sort of person who makes bread from mushy bananas and "mystery soup" from leftovers: I despise waste. I had *plans* for those 70+20 euros.

40. ˆ And not always even errors—despite being fully aware that I can get medical services for free, I once *chose* to pay for a private doctor for a checkup because she could speak English and I just couldn't bear the thought of trying to explain my medical history in Italian.

41. ˆ Okay, to be fair to sludge, which is basically a supernutrient smoothie... we still eat sludge some days and it's actually a really great, easy go-to meal that ensures we hit a minimum of real nutrients in a given day.

42. ˆ I know the phrase is the Lion's Share, but have you ever seen a documentary about lions? Lions are lazy SOBs, with lionesses taking care of all of the hunting, cub raising, etc. Though perhaps the phrase is meant to refer to how much the lazy SOB's eat compared to the amount they

contribute to the pride, which *would* be a lot? Whatever, I'm going with my first thought. So: lioness's share.

43. ^ And anyway, Ford's assembly line gave us all cars, but it also kinda kicked off the all-too-common practice of treating workers like cogs in a machine.

44. ^ Honestly, this is just a great general rule for life. Nothing good comes from eating or drinking after midnight, unless of course you are a consummate night owl and eight p.m. is breakfast.

45. ^ "No, my husband isn't *babysitting*. He's *parenting!!!*" - A frustrated friend.

46. ^ *Yes*, the German-raised part of me died a little inside writing that out. Trust me, Beware the Over Lean struggled for its place of pride in my go-to relationship guidelines: The idea of eschewing efficiency in favor of balance was hard-won territory in my brain.

47. ^ Please refer to the 80 percent rule.

48. ^ Fortunately, the nurse actually ended up speaking pretty decent English and I eventually recovered from COVID-19.

49. ^ We're not parents, but I imagine this is good practice for if you ever have kids, too.

50. ^ The funny thing is that, I have found the reverse presumption true for many of my European friends who are unhappy with *their* home countries, who seem to think that the US essentially operates either like 1950s Los Angeles or a 1980s suburb.

51. ^ Read: rapidly gentrifying.

52. ˆ Despite the fact that everyone in this conversation is, actually, an expat.

53. ˆ At least, it is if it grows into something more. Never let anyone make you feel like you're not worthy of true friendship!

54. ˆ It's not *not* one of the inspirations for this book...

55. ˆ True story: Adam and I realized that we may as well move overseas when a proposed move to a different neighborhood in his home city elicited a distressed response from one of his family members. Ultimately, there are some people who are simply never going to be happy with what you choose if it's not what they prescribe. You can spend your life trying to chase that dragon, or just do what makes you happy and deal with the fallout.

56. ˆ And perhaps the ability to not take things too seriously.

Ingram Content Group UK Ltd.
Milton Keynes UK
UKHW052208150323
418544UK00011B/106